Local Control
and
Accountability

Local Control
and
Accountability

How to Get It,
Keep It, and
Improve School
Performance

Richard Sagor

CORWIN PRESS, INC.
A Sage Publications Company
Thousand Oaks, California

For information address:

Corwin Press, Inc.
A Sage Publications Company
2455 Teller Road
Thousand Oaks, California 91320
e-mail: order@corwin.sagepub.com

SAGE Publications Ltd.
6 Bonhill Street
London EC2A 4PU
United Kingdom

SAGE Publications India Pvt. Ltd.
M-32 Market
Greater Kailash I
New Delhi 110 048 India

Printed in the United States of America

Library of Congress Cataloging-in-Publication Data

Sagor, Richard.
    Local control and accountability: How to get it, keep it, and improve school performance / Richard Sagor.
        p. cm.
    Includes bibliographical references (pp. 119-120) and index.
    ISBN 0-8039-6411-0 (cloth: acid-free paper). — ISBN
0-8039-6412-9 (pbk.: acid-free paper)
        1. Educational accountability—United States. 2. Schools—
Decentralization—United States.   I. Title.
LB2806.22.S25   1996
379.1'54—dc20   96-10082

This book is printed on acid-free paper.

       98 99 00 10 9 8 7 6 5 4 3 2

Production Editor: Sherrise Purdum
Typesetter/Designer: Rebecca Evans/Tina Hill
Cover Designer: Marcia R. Finlayson

Contents

Preface

I distinctly remember the debates I had with myself over the use of the term "accountability" in the title of this book. Accountability has become a tough, value-laden, even hostile word in the education vocabulary.

For too many educators, it carries connotations of power being exerted over them by external quality control officers. We are reminded of politicians, administrators, or demagogues promising to hold others accountable for the results of their performance. It is truly unfortunate that such an important concept has had to carry all of this negative baggage. However, after much consideration, I came to realize that no synonym, regardless of its political correctness, would be appropriate.

The accountability function that is at the heart of this book is also at the heart of professional practice. It is, in fact, what separates the work of professionals from that of other workers. Supervisors hold workers accountable for doing each element of their jobs effectively. Professionals, on the other hand, hold themselves accountable for the end products of their endeavors. Professionals feel inextricably connected to their work. They do not simply carry out tasks, but seek to produce final outcomes in which they can take pride and that will serve their clients well.

When discussing self-governance, Linda Darling-Hammond (1988) argues that three prerequisites define professional work:

1. Knowledge of those principles, theories, and factors that undergird appropriate decisions about which procedures should be employed—and knowledge of the procedures themselves.
2. The ability to apply this knowledge in nonroutine circumstances, taking relevant circumstances into account.
3. A commitment to do what is best for the client, not what is easiest or most expedient.

I agree with Darling-Hammond, and for this reason, I believe that nothing is more important to educational reform than making the practice of teaching fully "professional." This includes reinforcing the professional ethic of holding ourselves to the highest standards of performance as well as customer satisfaction. That is why this book is embracing the language of accountability, not as something to be done to educators but as something in which educators should feel compelled to engage for the sake of their students.

As you read through this book, you will encounter analogy after analogy contrasting the professions of teaching and medicine. This is done with full knowledge that there is much that could or should be done to reform the health professions. However, because most people in our society see American medicine as a field that succeeds in carrying out its mission with high levels of expertise, it provides us with many analogies worth contemplating. I need to explain two other particular editorial decisions to the reader before proceeding any further.

First, this book makes heavy use of case studies to illustrate the principles and techniques available to the site-based managed school. Early on, I made a decision to use neither hypothetical examples nor representations of specific schools. Rather, I chose to build these case studies using carefully drawn composites from schools that were making regular use of the techniques of data-based decision making. I did this because I wished to offer proposals that were grounded in reality and more than mere suppositions on my part, yet I wanted each example to correspond tightly to the specific principles being discussed in each chapter. My only regret in using the composites is that the many creative educators who taught me the methods reported in this book (and appropriately attributed to the composite schools) are identified by pseudonyms, and these innovative educators thus have been denied the opportunity to publicly take the bows they so richly deserve. To all of you who see yourselves in this book, please accept my sincere and hearty thank you.

Second, throughout the text I use the term "faculty" as synonymous with the schools' key stakeholders. In no way should this be interpreted as an inference that teachers should be the only party with a say in local school governance. Nothing could be further from the truth. I decided to use the term "faculty" because teachers are the one common denominator in all approaches to site-based decision making. The faculty has a voice in every locally controlled school that I've encountered. However, in most cases, the voices of students, parents, and patrons are also heard and included in the local decision-making process. The reader should feel free (and is even encouraged) to expand the term "faculty" to include all local stakeholders who have been delegated a part in decision making at their local schools.

Nothing in our recent history has made the need and the potential for self-imposed accountability more important than the movement toward site-based management (SBM). The unifying feature of all SBM efforts is to put more control and power in the hands of those closest to the work. When SBM works, it clearly provides efficient and responsive approaches to the problems facing our public schools. However, we already have enough data to alert us to the fact that SBM isn't foolproof. In fact, each week, we are hearing more and more reports that SBM simply doesn't work.

Some of the best research on locally controlled (SBM) schools has been conducted by Priscilla Wohlstetter and her colleagues at the University of Southern California's School Based Management Project. In their work, they have succeeded in isolating a set of factors that appears to distinguish the successful SBM efforts from the failures. These include the following:

1. People at the site must exercise authority
2. This authority must be used to affect teaching and learning
3. Professional development must focus on the development of problem-solving skills

4. Adequate information dissemination systems must be in place and are critical to school success
5. A viable reward system must be in place that recognizes improved performance

This book has been designed to provide specific examples of strategies that schools have used successfully to accomplish each of the five critical elements cited by Wohlstetter and to enhance their quality control and accountability functions.

A final reason for bringing the term "accountability" out of the closet at this time is the growing acceptance by schools of the techniques of the total quality movement. The work of W. Edwards Deming and his colleagues is beginning to have a profound impact on schools as well as many other institutions. For those of us working in the public schools, it could be argued that the essence of total quality lies in our finding and/or creating ways to organize our professional colleagues to use data in their pursuit of continuous progress. Simply put, this is the task that confronts any individual or group of individuals that is attempting to make SBM successful for the clients of its school.

In schools that have implemented the technologies of total quality and have consequently exhibited the conditions that research finds necessary for successful SBM, accountability ceases to be seen as a negative term. In fact, increased accountability becomes the best explanation for why these schools are enjoying such unparalleled support from the communities they serve.

It is my most sincere hope that this book will assist readers in their search for ways to bring high levels of success as well as political support to the schools in which they work.

About the Author

Richard Sagor has 14 years of public school administrative experience, including service as an assistant superintendent, a high school principal, an instruction vice principal, a disciplinary vice principal, and an alternative school head teacher. He has taught students—from the gifted to the learning disabled—in the areas of social studies, reading, and written composition. Educated in the public schools of New York, Dick received his BA degree from New York University before moving to the Pacific Northwest, where he earned two MA degrees and a PhD in curriculum and instruction from the University of Oregon.

In addition to his work as a teacher and an administrator, Dick has extensive consulting experience, having served as a site visitor for the U.S. Department of Education's Secondary School Recognition Program and as a consultant to state departments of education and dozens of local school districts around the country on leadership, data-based school improvement, student motivation, and programming for at-risk youth. His articles on education, school reform, and action research have received awards from the National Association of Secondary School Principals and the Educational Press Association of America. Dick's most recent books include *The TQE Principal:*

A Transformed Leader, At-Risk Students: Reaching and Teaching Them, and *How to Conduct Collaborative Action Research.*

Dick is an Associate Professor of Educational Administration at Washington State University, working out of the branch campus in Vancouver, Washington. In addition to his teaching duties, Dick directs Project LEARN (League of Educational Action Researchers in the Northwest) and is the founding director of the Southwest Washington Collaborative Professional Development School. Project LEARN is a consortium of schools and districts that believes that school performance is best enhanced through the collaborative work of the professional staff. The "Collaborative Professional Development Schools" that he founded are joint ventures of Washington State University and several area school districts. This project has been an attempt to develop new paradigms for the professional development of educators while fostering the renewal of schools.

1

Why Be Concerned About Accountability?

Seldom in our history has there been a greater opportunity afforded to those pursuing school reform. Although some educators may differ with my rosy assertion (mainly because of the painful retrenchments that are accompanying budget reductions around the country), I remain confident that, on this issue, I am right. It is because of a peculiar and often overlooked phenomenon—specifically, the near unanimous national (perhaps even worldwide) infatuation with local control.

In this current era, it seems that everyone agrees that "less is more," or its corollary, "smaller is bigger." We can see this everywhere: in the social disintegration of geographic regions as diverse as the Balkans, with the breakaway movement of the Quebec separatists, and with the constituent republics of the old Soviet Union. This is not just an international phenomenon. We also see it in domestic educational policy: in the accelerating momentum pushing toward greater local authority with a consequent diminution of Washington's role; in the weakening of our state educational bureaucracies; in the strengthening of site-based management (SBM) schemes; and in the push for local control of schools, the content of curriculum, and the policies that affect the daily lives of our children.

1

The sources of this shift are many, and the explanations for its ascension are equally varied (for a full discussion of this phenomenon, especially as a "Mega-Trend," the reader is advised to look elsewhere), but the positive impact that this could have on public education could be phenomenal—that is, if we seize this opportunity!

I'll elaborate. For the past 40 years, it has been an almost unchallenged dogma that for serious quality control to occur, it had to be external. This is because it was believed that larger centralized entities were in a better position to plan for a glorious future than were many diffuse, underfunded, uncoordinated, and parochial local constituencies. This belief system gave birth to larger governments, larger and more complex school systems, greater divisions of authority, and, for the classroom teacher and local schools, far more regulatory control than had ever before been experienced.

It is, however, important to understand that this didn't happen as a result of a conspiracy of evil forces; rather, it was born of a very reasonable public expectation: high-quality performance! In the industrial age (ever since Eli Whitney's cotton gin), it was presumed that specialization, lines of control, and bureaucracy were the best and most logical ways to ensure efficient production of quality products. In retrospect, our collective faith in "the system" was probably misplaced. Overwhelmingly, the public, both here and abroad, has come to believe that organizational complexity and top-down regulatory control are big parts of the problem rather than the source of our salvation.

As a consequence, the left (liberals) and the right (conservatives) have found unusual agreement in the proposition that local control of social services (decentralization) is the best strategy if we truly want services of "high quality." In short, the now-prevailing view is that those closest to the action and those with the greatest stake in immediate outcomes are the ones in the best position to hold their institutions and organizations accountable.

For those of us in education, this has meant a decided preference for site-based initiatives and strategies aimed at empowering teachers and local educators to take greater control over the direction of their schools. Progressives have found this an attractive philosophy because they believe that schools exist primarily to serve local constituencies, and they want to devolve power to the communities that are being served. More conservative groups find this approach attractive because they are naturally suspicious of big government and centralized bureaucracy. For whatever reason, it is both a strange and wondrous moment when both extremes of our political spectrum seem to agree on a strategy—in this case, that schools will work better if those who have the greatest investment in them—the children, the parents, and the local educators—are given a greater voice in the governance and decision making that affects their schools.

I have come to the same conclusion. In my case, it wasn't due to ideology but rather my thinking about what contributes to quality instruction. I have found, and the research that I've read confirms, that in the schools where faculty behavior reflects accepted definitions of professionalism, the children prosper. Conversely, in those schools where the instructors tend to see themselves as blue-collar workers or as employees who are simply fulfilling routinized job descriptions, the children tend to benefit less from their schooling experience. For this reason, I feel it behooves us to pause and examine the essential components of professionalism.

The Essential Elements of Professional Practice

What Are the Attributes of Professional Practice?

We know certain things about professionals, and these understandings are reinforced wherever and whenever we see them working. Professionals exercise a certain degree of autonomy; they demonstrate mastery of a body of knowledge that meaningfully informs their practice; they contribute to the development of their knowledge base; and they tend to look to themselves, their peers, and their clients for affirmation and assessment.

For example, lawyers design their own trial strategies, informed by precedents set by other lawyers; their professional experiences (both successes and failures) add to the body of knowledge that informs legal practice; and our society celebrates the lawyers who are known to have achieved the highest levels of competence.

The same applies in engineering and architecture. Original patents and designs are generated by individuals and teams of engineers, whereas each additional improvement adds to the body of knowledge on how one should design and construct buildings, machines, or appliances.

Likewise with medicine, we witness the same phenomena consistently. Doctors select treatment regimens based upon the findings of other doctors, and the results obtained by their patients add to the medical literature. So, what is the experience of teachers?

Unlike other professionals, but like blue-collar workers, teachers are generally told what and how to teach and how they should assess the consequences of their interventions, and then they are subjected to the judgment of administrators or supervisors on how good of a job they have done. You might be asking, So what? What if teaching is more akin to blue-collar work than professional pursuits? Why does it matter? The "so what?" is the impact it is having on student performance!

When professionals feel empowered and responsible for their decisions, they tend to hold themselves to high standards of performance. Likewise, when workers feel subjected to arbitrary and external standards, they will tend to give up personal responsibility for their performance and the outcomes of the production process. Workers tend to adjust easily to doing no more than what they are told. Thus, if and when low performance occurs, the onus for explaining or correcting it ends up as the obligation of the supervisor and/or overseer.

So where does that place us at this most propitious time? On one hand, our society is distrustful of the ability of the hierarchical structures we have built to ensure quality control and therefore seems anxious to devolve decision making to lower levels of the educational totem pole. Unfortunately, those residing at the lower levels of the organizational structure (the teachers) have become conditioned to following the orders of their bosses—those people the system has deemed "smarter and wiser" than the teachers themselves. As a consequence, too many teachers dutifully implement the prescriptions of others and are forced to accept the judgment that others make of their performance. So who benefits from this sorry state of affairs? If my perception is correct, the answer is, Almost no one!

What we have created is a public education system, once the envy of the world, that now is clearly the subject of widespread derision. So why do I declare it to be a propitious moment of opportunity? Because a phoenix can rise out of these ashes. It is most certainly an opportunity, but it is also a unique moment that can and might be squandered if we are not careful. Readers of the emerging literature on site-based management (SBM) have observed what is, at best, a mixed picture. Many decentralized systems have not only failed to produce improved performance but in a number of urban cases, student performance has continued to decline. I fear this is because in far too many cases, all that SBM amounted to was a governance change, a highly touted tinkering with who will make which decisions. Instead, what schools really need is meaningful change both in the very nature of the decisions themselves and in the criteria upon which decisions are actually made.

Those who have lived through a number of educational cycles (fads, as many cynics like to call them) may see this "movement" as simply another pendulum swing. A most predictable time, where frustration with centralization and bureaucratic control gave way to the more primal urge for local control and decentralization, ultimately to be followed by inevitable frustration with what the new order brought, finally ushering in yet another backlash. But history does not have to repeat itself. We can seize the opportunity. We can produce an educational system that works for the children it serves, and thus stop the swinging pendulum right in its tracks! But what it will take is a commitment to an age-old, and too often denigrated, principle: personal and collective accountability.

One of the side benefits of the current educational system is that the higher-ups (be they administrators, school board members, or legislators) have been the only ones held accountable. Principals and superintendents were the ones fired when their schools failed to perform. Boards of education, governors, and state legislatures were asked to account for tax dollars that didn't provide high enough quality for students. Even though they were often ridiculed in the press, most local educators could dodge the blame or at least avoid the primary responsibility for fixing the system. They could always claim, "It is the fault of those stupid unfunded mandates from the board, the state capitol, and/or Washington, DC!"

With no one to hold accountable, it is no wonder that our system has been seen by so many as a failure. No wonder that the prevailing viewpoint is that power should be stripped from the hierarchy and redistributed to the "lowerarchy." But will changing the locus of power automatically change school performance? That is, in my opinion, a very naive expectation. Just changing who makes which decisions won't change systemic performance; it will only postpone the day when the patrons will rise up again and vent their frustrations anew, this time blaming the "site-councils" (or whichever group is in charge) and reinvesting control back with the higher-ups. Yes, the cycle may seem all but inevitable unless we take action and we take it now!

Schools engaged in SBM and other decentralization strategies can choose to take quality control to heart. Rather than focusing solely on who makes the decisions and the mechanics of decision making, they can remake themselves as professional "learning organizations" (Senge, 1990)—places where decisions are made by professionals based upon the accumulation of relevant, local, and contextually sensitive data. Such a change, I suspect, would produce a wave of public confidence unparalleled in education's history.

To bring this point home, I offer a not-so-far-fetched analogy. Consider your previous visit to the family doctor, a person in whom you probably invest considerable confidence. How is professional decision making carried out by this physician? Did he or she prescribe for you what his or her supervisor said to? Does your family doctor always go by the book, or does your doctor approach each medical condition this way:

> Let's try this. I've been having good luck with treatments like this with patients like you, and I'd like to try it for a few weeks. Then why don't you come back, we'll see how you are doing, and reassess our approach to your treatment at that time.

That is how my doctor works with me, and I'm glad she does! I, for one, trust doctors far more who consider my unique needs, in light of their past experience and knowledge, and then create new prescriptions accordingly. In such cases, I feel not only that my unique needs and circumstances are being considered but also that a continually evolving and relevant knowledge base is influencing the doctor's decisions on my behalf.

More important, I know that each of my doctor's further actions will be informed by valid and reliable data on my individual progress and not by some textbook definition on how I should be progressing. In the world in which my doctor works, my (the patient's) confidence is high and my doctor's (the professional's) morale and sense of efficacy are strong.

This is the opportunity before us. As public school educators, we can remake our practice following a professional paradigm. We can seize the opportunity, not simply to take the power that is being delegated to us, but to recommit ourselves to carrying out our professional decisions and to constructing our decision-making processes in a totally new light. The purpose of this book is to help educators do just that.

Many schools across North America have found ways to become what Carl Glickman (1993) and others refer to as self-renewing schools. In doing so, these schools have fostered professional environments where

- High expectations prevail
- Collegiality is the norm
- Experimentation is a constant (Sagor, 1995)

In the chapters that follow, we will get to know some of these self-renewing schools, and we will examine the strategies that have assisted them in achieving high levels of student performance. We will see how they have built norms of professional practice for teachers, all the while inspiring confidence in the communities they serve. We will notice that by taking charge of the "quality control function"—something often called "accountability"—these schools have, in fact, transformed themselves. They have become beacons—visions of what all of America's schools could become if we choose to take advantage of the unprecedented opportunity before us. These schools show us what to expect if we bring wisdom and strength to this opportunity to control the fate of our society's most important institution, the one charged with bringing up our community's children.

How Are Decisions Made Now?
What Should Change?

The decision-making structure in most schools is crystal clear. The disgruntled parent or patron always knows where to direct his or her complaints. They go right to the boss. But what about the concerns of the educators themselves? How are issues traditionally resolved by the faculties working inside our schools?

In the best of schools, we are told that decisions are made democratically, but we should not confuse that with being made competently or professionally. If the majority of a faculty holds a bias toward an instructional strategy and that strategy is not in the best interest of the students, by a democratic vote, this treatment could be imposed on the kids. Would any of us like to empower a hospital staff to have a vote on continuing the use of a discredited treatment for their patients? I think not! We trust and assume that our medical professionals make decisions based upon pertinent data about us (their patients) as well as knowledge about how those conditions might be affecting us.

Biased-Based Decision Making

I believe that if we honestly assess how decisions are currently made by the faculty in most schools, we will see that decision making frequently falls into what might be called a "biased-based" decisional framework. We tend to lobby our colleagues to get their approval of our predilections, be it ability grouping or detracking, whole language or phonics, or inclusion or resource rooms. Then, based on the effectiveness of our lobbying and the persuasiveness of our opponents, a vote is taken and a majority position emerges. But is "biased-based" decision making always in the best interest of our students? And even when it is in the best interest of most of the students, is it good for each one of them?

Again, I'll enlist the medical model. The democratic model of schooling has caused us to worship at the altar of "central tendency." Central tendency is a statistical concept that makes a great deal of sense. Its power comes from a history of quantitative research that seeks to discern what works best for the overwhelming majority of subjects. I don't object to this research model; rather, I blame its overapplication.

Examining an issue of significant public concern might prove helpful here. Were we to look closely at the research on grade-level retention, we would find a decisive body of evidence that suggests that this strategy is frequently detrimental. I suspect a meta-analysis on retention might even show that three out of four students who are retained at grade level are likely to suffer deleterious effects from that intervention. Looking at such powerful evidence of central tendency, it is no surprise that policy makers are becoming weary of the retention intervention. In fact, we can find many schools and districts where, based on this evidence, the practice of grade-level retention has been banned. This example hardly looks like poor biased-based decision making, does it? After all, these policies are based on a substantial body of research. But, upon professional scrutiny, can we say that the research really supports this approach?

I think not. Let's examine the research closely. Although it is certainly clear that most young people fail to sustain benefits from being retained, is that true of all retained students? Clearly not. Even the most critical findings suggest that some students do, in fact, receive benefits from this intervention. Yet our habit of adhering religiously to the central tendency argument has caused us to decree that what is good for most must, by necessity, be good for all. Does that make sense?

Let's return for a moment to medicine. Penicillin effectively fights off infections with most patients, but how would we feel about

a hospital that adopted penicillin as the treatment for all of its patients, regardless of their medical history or allergic propensities? I
think we would say such a hospital is an example of bureaucracy
gone mad! Furthermore, we would be appalled by the abdication of
professional decision making on the part of the medical staff. That is
precisely the way many students and parents have come to see decision making in many of our schools today.

How do we get around the burden of central tendency and the
habits of behaving as if "one size will fit all"? I suggest we do this in
the same manner as scientists have done in other fields. Using the
example of the family doctor from the first chapter, we can begin to
see where education should be headed.

Instinctively, when a doctor tells us that a particular treatment is
guaranteed to succeed with us, we are intuitively suspicious. If you
are like me, you invest far more credibility in the physician who says
something like,

> I have had considerable luck with patients with a similar
> profile to you with this treatment. For that reason I'd like to
> give it a try. What do you say we go with it for a few weeks
> and then come back in? If it is working, we will keep with it.
> If not, that would be a good time to consider a change.

When my doctor says this, it inspires confidence. It does so because in expressing her uncertainty, my doctor is acknowledging that
no two patients could possibly possess the same physiology. Her consideration of me as an individual gives me both comfort and confidence. Now consider the feelings of the typical parent whose child is
having difficulty with reading. Suppose the school's position is,

> We've spent the past year studying a variety of approaches
> to the teaching of reading. After careful analysis, our lan-
> guage arts committee has decided that the best approach is
> 'whole language.' We have confidence in our committee, so
> you shouldn't worry about Emma's success in our reading
> program.

As a parent, I would get little comfort from this position. It's not
that I don't trust the faculty nor that I think they didn't approach their
task of studying alternative approaches to reading seriously and ob-

jectively. Rather, I am suspicious of the "one size fits all" bias inherent in this approach to program adoption.

If doctors are comfortable in declaring that each patient is unique, with all that our physical attributes have in common, is it too much to ask that schools and teachers recognize the individual characteristics of learners when choosing their interventions?

The Love Affair With Consensus

A related problem in our decision-making processes is our infatuation with consensus. When one looks at school improvement efforts around the country, one could suspect that the virtues of reaching consensus appeared on the stone tablets that Moses brought down from Mount Sinai.

In many SBM schools, you will hear it asserted as a major tenet that "We make decisions by consensus. We never vote!" On the surface, that sounds good. Who could find fault with honest deliberations and efforts to include everyone in the process. Furthermore, it seems logical that agreement will bring commitment. But the essential problem lies in using a strategy aimed at the often naive hope of conflict "resolution" rather than using a more realistic and beneficial approach—namely, one aimed at conflict "management." It is important that, as professionals, we understand the difference between conflict resolution and management. Let me elaborate.

In all but inconsequential issues, it is to be expected that differing viewpoints will exist, especially in a pursuit that frequently is called more of an art than a science. When it comes to teaching, reasonable people can be expected to differ on strategies. Equally moral and committed people, all with the interest of handicapped learners in their hearts, could well differ on the best strategy for serving these kids: inclusion or resource room (this example is explored at length in Chapter 7). Likewise, caring educators could find room for disagreement on the best approaches for teaching reading, science, government, and the arts. Why, then, do we so often push for consensus? I think it is because we see it as a way to reduce conflict. This it certainly does, but it accomplishes this at a tremendous cost; forcing consensus often comes at the expense of commitment and passion.

Pushing for the one and only solution to which we can all agree is akin to selecting a single color we all will like equally. Because we could never reach agreement on bold colors (some of us love red, others love blue, etc.), we will inevitably end up going along with some bland choice like beige or off-white. In schools that worship at the altar of consensus, too many teachers have learned to "go along to get along." Agreement is often reached on the most innocuous proposal, the one everybody "can live with." Unfortunately, we also end up with something about which no one seems to care very much. I fear this is way too high a price to pay for peace.

Are There Alternatives?

One reason that consensus has become so appealing to educators is that it appears that the only alternative is a majority rule decision. We all know the pitfalls here! Even when we get a substantial majority—a two-thirds vote (why, that is even enough to pass a constitutional amendment!)—a controversial decision is likely to fail. Would anyone seriously want to adopt a reading series when one third of the faculty is opposed to it? We all know a small and vocal minority can sink any ship! Well, is majority rule the only alternative to consensus? Successful, self-renewing schools have taught us that the answer is no!

Return once again to the medical metaphor. When a hospital can't reach consensus on a single antibiotic, they don't postpone their decision; rather, they allow alternative approaches (existing treatments) so that additional data can be collected on their relative efficacy. If one medicine ultimately shows itself to be demonstrably superior for all patients (e.g., the Sabin polio vaccine), then it is adopted for use with everyone. As is more often the case, if multiple approaches appear to be helpful, depending on circumstances, then they continue to coexist and are prescribed discriminately.

Would it be the end of the world if a school chose to teach phonics and whole language? Had resource rooms and practiced inclusion? Had multiaged and single-aged classroom configurations? I doubt it. In fact, in a study of several schools that had successfully "overcome the one-solution syndrome" and produced programs that were deemed highly effective, the rejection of consensus was observed as one of the more salient features of decision making (Sagor, 1995).

In the remaining chapters, we will see how schools have moved from their old habits of biased-based decision making to data-based decision making. We will see how, by doing so, they have forged strategies to overcome the burdens of consensus and the one-solution syndrome. But the most exciting part is that we will see how in managing this dilemma, these schools have become happier and more productive places for students, teachers, and parents.

The Three Building Blocks of Accountability

Vision Setting, Action Research, and Performance Assessment

School leaders concerned with site-based school improvement have invested increasingly in three separate yet closely related endeavors: vision setting, action research, and performance assessment.

It has become almost axiomatic to assert that serious efforts at school reform need to begin with a clear and compelling "shared vision." Peter Senge (1990) has even argued that learning how to shape shared visions is one of the five critical "disciplines" of effective leadership. We often hear those advocating local control, enumerating the benefits to be obtained when teachers actively participate in research on their own practice. Many in the educational community are holding that the role of teacher must be expanded to include the job of "performance assessor."

Those interested in bringing accountability and continuous progress to locally controlled schools are finding that when these three areas (vision setting, action research, and performance assessment) are fully and properly integrated, they become a force for dramatically accelerated school improvement.

Collaborative Action Research and Performance Assessment

Before delving into how these two themes should be woven together, it will prove helpful to examine the many fundamental elements that they hold in common. Most efforts at performance assessment and approaches to teacher-conducted action research are based upon the following assumptions.

To be maximally useful for educators at a local site:

1. Performance data need to be collected and analyzed by local practitioners.
2. Instrumentation and data collection methods need to be sensitive to the unique aspects of the local context.
3. Multiple sources of data (triangulation) should be used to establish validity and reliability.
4. The attainment of educational outcomes should be understood as the consequence of a number of interrelated variables.

Collaborative Action Research

Ever since Kurt Lewin began writing about it in the 1940s, schools have engaged in collaborative action research for a multitude of reasons. Among those cited are virtues embedded in the process itself (Elliott, 1981; Oja & Smulyan, 1989), the synergy created when collegial groups work together conducting disciplined inquiries into issues of their own professional practice (Holly & Southworth, 1989; Schaefer, 1967), and the generation of a professional knowledge base (Griffen et al., 1983; Tikunoff & Ward, 1983). A review of the literature shows that collaborative action research has been credited with supporting a variety of professional virtues. Among the benefits produced by the pursuit of action research are teacher development (Glickman, 1988; Hargreaves & Fullan, 1992), team/school development (Calhoun, 1994; Joyce, Wolf, & Calhoun, 1993), and program development. Clearly, all of these virtues are needed in locally controlled schools.

However, what haven't been explored widely (up until now) are the political benefits of this work. If SBM schools are to maintain and/or expand their decision-making authority, they will need to harness the tools of assessment and action research and use them to build public support for their initiatives. Later in this chapter and throughout this book, we will see how "local control" schools have derived considerable political leverage based on their action research.

Applied Performance Assessment

Not unlike action research, applied performance assessment has been receiving widespread interest because of the array of virtues embedded in this technology (Stiggins, 1994; Wiggins, 1993). Educators, as well as students and parents, have begun accepting the fact that the skills needed and desired for students extend well beyond the academic objectives that can be reliably assessed through norm-referenced testing, and with the growing acknowledgment that schooling should be relevant (designed around authentic tasks), the development of applied performance assessment systems is being seen as essential.

The reason we need to connect the action research and assessment strategies becomes evident when one examines the recent efforts to implement performance-based education. A casual observer might view the rising interest in student performance by educators to be a new wave of innovation. Actually, educators' interest in helping their students attain skills is nothing new. In fact, I would argue that it is really slanderous to contend otherwise. Of course, teachers have always been driven to enhance the knowledge and skills obtained by their students! I believe that the real reason that the performance focus appears as a paradigm shift is that policy makers and school administrators alike decided it was time to refocus energy on the products (outcomes) produced by students, rather than the processes and strategies in which their teachers are engaged.

Although it may be true that concern about performance outcomes isn't new, it is also fair to admit that our collective concern about student performance, albeit widespread, has not resulted, up until now, in the quantity, quality, or level of student learning that the public has rightfully demanded. The key question that this history of lower (than hoped for) performance should raise for reformers is, Why?

Why Have Traditional Educational Practices Kept Us From Achieving More Impressive Outcomes?

One possible, although politically incorrect, answer could be teacher incompetence. Obviously, if America's teachers suffered from a gross inability to teach, it would result in a decline in student performance. Another argument that is kinder and gentler places the blame on professional complacency. The logic of this argument is that although America's teachers may have professed a sincere commitment to produce high levels of student performance, their dedication to this goal hasn't run very deep.

I believe, however, that most fair and honest observers of America's public schools would conclude that we have not suffered from an overabundance of incompetent teachers, nor have our teachers' stated professional concerns for student success been insincere. Rather, I think, a fair evaluation of our schools' failure to produce uniformly high levels of performance on meaningful "outcomes" would show that this state of affairs has resulted from an almost universal absence of contextually sensitive, meaningful data on the performance of both teachers and learners.

We might then ask, Why have our centrally managed schools failed to collect such data? It appears to be the result of several factors:

First, in big systems, it has been hard to achieve clarity on the specific outcomes that local schools wished to pursue.

Second, schools have not had the means (instruments) to be sure when and if desired outcomes were obtained.

Third, schools have not chosen to assess the relative benefits of competing instructional strategies for their students.

These three oversights compound each other and contribute to other significant problems. In fact, I believe they are responsible for a large part of the current public distrust and concern about our schools. But that is not all!

Our students have suffered because their performance has been less than it should be. Furthermore, teachers have been denied the job satisfaction that could accompany valid and reliable feedback on the success of their work. But perhaps the most damaging consequence of the absence of valid and reliable data on our teaching is political. In education (as in most policy areas), the one who controls the data controls the discourse. The lack of good data to bring to the table has diminished the credibility of the teacher's voice on policy issues to that of a special interest group rather than the wisdom of a community of informed professionals.

The relevance of this to SBM schools is great because if the voice of teachers in locally controlled schools becomes seen as simply self-interest, then their voice in governance will be short-lived! To support this argument, I ask the reader to consider the following scenario:

What If . . . ?

Imagine that the teachers in your local community were able to articulate clearly which performance outcomes (both affective and cognitive) were desired for the students. Furthermore, imagine that these teachers not only were capable of reporting accurately on the *authentic* attainment of these outcomes by the students but also could, with credibility, demonstrate the relationship between the interventions (teaching strategies and programs) used and the student outcomes achieved. Would we expect morale to be high and for these teachers to be professionally fulfilled? Furthermore, wouldn't we expect the patrons of this district to be willing to invest considerable confidence in their teaching staff and to be open to delegating more authority to them?

I believe most of us would answer yes to each of the above questions. But to make this scenario true for all locally controlled (SBM) schools, we will need to link vision setting, action research, and performance assessment. When fully integrated, these approaches enable practitioners to work collaboratively toward the attainment of four critical goals:

1. Achieving clarity on the outcomes sought from teaching
2. Identifying multiple sources of data on outcome attainment

3. Articulating the theories (assumptions) that are held about how desired outcomes are to be facilitated (taught)
4. Identifying multiple sources of data on the viability of our teaching (implementation strategies)

1. *Achieving clarity on the outcomes sought from teaching.* By clarity I am referring to "communicable" clarity, the ability to inform parents, patrons, and policy makers, in terms that will be appreciated and understood, exactly what a successful student will be able to demonstrate as a consequence of his or her schooling experience.
2. *Identifying multiple sources of data on outcome attainment.* Whereas some academic outcomes might be measured validly and reliably with a single measurement (e.g., the addition of three-digit numbers), many desirable goals can be validly assessed only through multiple sources (triangulated data collection). For example, if our goal is for students to develop a love of reading, test scores alone simply can't provide a complete answer, nor would responses on an opinion survey be enough to satisfy a skeptic. Yet test scores augmented by survey data and further correlated with reading logs and library circulation records can produce a picture with both construct and face validity.
3. *Articulating the theories (assumptions) that are held about how desired outcomes are to be facilitated (taught).* Unless we want to plead guilty to the charge of perpetuating superstitions, we need to be able to justify our choice of instructional strategies with reasoned theories on their value. Failure to do so can result in our perpetuating practices that add no value, while at the same time causing us to neglect approaches with potentially significant impact.
4. *Identify multiple sources of data on the viability of our teaching (implementation strategies).* If we are going to draw conclusions on the relative merits of the strategies that we are employing, the validity and reliability of the data informing those judgments must be as strong as possible. In most cases, no single source of data could be powerful enough to justify the continuation or cessation of a particular strategy, especially if that strategy is part of a lengthy causal chain. For these reasons, decisions on instructional strategies need to be informed by multiple sources (triangulation) of data.

Imagine that it is 5 years from now. Your school has been successful beyond even your highest expectations. It is the last week of May, and you are witnessing a student going through a significant rite of passage: the school's exit exhibition. This is a 20-minute oral presentation (accompanied by artifacts if and when necessary) given before a panel of six adults (the student's parents, two teachers, and two "at-large" community members).

The student's assignment is to

- Describe/demonstrate the skills or knowledge that he or she has developed as a consequence of his or her educational experience
- Explain/demonstrate how the skills or knowledge was acquired

Describe in whatever voice you find appropriate the scene you see unfolding:

Figure 3.1. Prompt

Putting It All Together

Integrating vision setting, action research, and performance assessment requires that school improvement teams at SBM schools follow a four-step process. Each step is designed to address one of the goals delineated above.

Step 1, achieving "communicable" clarity on outcomes sought, can be achieved in a number of ways. Many of the schools with which I've worked have had success with a "backward planning" approach that we call "scenario writing." At a faculty meeting, using the following prompt (Figure 3.1), teachers are asked to author a personal success story.

Individual writing is then followed by collective editing. Teachers are invited to share those elements of their "visions" that they find attractive. The composite scenarios that emerge assist the faculty in achieving communicable clarity on the outcomes with which they are most concerned. More important, this process is done in terms that become intelligible to students, parents, and patrons. Often, the resulting school scenarios are as much as five single-spaced pages of text. Figure 3.2 is an illustration of a portion of one school's scenario.

Ellisa walks confidently to the front of the room, where a display table is neatly arranged with artwork, a science apparatus, and books. Clearly, the books are dominating the display. Ellisa clears her throat and begins her presentation. After welcoming us and thanking us for taking the time to join her on this special occasion, she jumps right into the business of the day. Using the computer-generated displays on the overhead projector, she outlines for us the goals of her presentation. She tells us that

1. I want you to become familiar with me, my goals, and the experiences I've had at Speakeasy Middle School.
2. I want you to take a brief look at the products that I am most proud of and have placed in my school portfolio.
3. I want you to understand the goals I have set for myself.

Having completed her introduction, she tells us of the shy, self-conscious, awkward girl who came to Speakeasy as a sixth grader, a mere 3 years ago. Smiling, she says, "While you might find it hard to believe, I was petrified to speak in front of a group back then." She explains that all of that began to change in the fall of her first year at Speakeasy. She gives much of the credit to Mrs. Plimkin, her teacher/advisor. She recounts for us how it all began with an advisory project that her group wrote and performed as part of the Columbus Day assembly. Her group wanted to portray the exploration of the New World from the perspective of the Native Americans.

She tells us of her fear upon being chosen to deliver the emotional conclusion to the assembly. But Mrs. Plimkin assured her she could do it better than anyone else. At this point, she invites us to look at the television monitor, and she plays a 2-minute video of her portion of the assembly. As we watch the video, we can see her adult demeanor fade a bit. She is clearly embarrassed to watch others see her on the screen. As the tape ends, she composes herself and continues.

After the assembly, she felt that everyone saw her differently, and she began volunteering more, both in class and in her after-school activities. She picks up a pile of programs (from three school plays and seven assemblies where she played key roles) and passes them around for our review. She goes on to say that although overcoming her shyness and becoming a performer has been fun, there is much more to her than performing. "In reality," she says, "I am still a quiet person. I am someone who likes to read and think through things before I talk too much about them. I think that is why science has become such an obsession for me."

Figure 3.2. Speakeasy School Scenario

She tells us that at Speakeasy, every student can select two elective classes every term. On the overhead, she now displays the classes she has taken over the 4 years, highlighting in pink her electives. It is easy for us to see that when given the choice, Ellisa seems to gravitate toward science. She tells us that although some people accuse her of trying to be like her older brother, a science major at the state university, she says it has nothing to do with that. "All right, maybe it has a little to do with trying to impress him, but I do really love doing experiments!"

She then draws our attention to the apparatus on the table in the front of the room. She explains that this is the mock-up of her design to powering our community with a mixture of solar- and wind-generated power. After a quick review of the apparatus, she again draws our attention to the television, where we watch a 3-minute segment of her presenting her energy project at last year's science fair.

Gazing at the clock, she sees that time is marching on, so she shifts into a discussion of her future plans. She assures us this will definitely include science, but it may also involve her interests in writing. This brings her to the book display. She begins by telling us of her interest in writing, which traces back to elementary school. Drawing our attention to the stack of colorful books before her, she shares that these were all books that she wrote, edited, and published in elementary school. Although she declares that "they really are very childish," we can see that she still has pride in her earlier work. But this brings her to tell us excitedly of her newfound love, writing science fiction.

She points out that in front of her on the table are books by H. G. Wells, Jules Verne, and Isaac Asimov. She says that they were all great "in their time," but because of the school's new technology lab, she is able to produce works with much more sophistication. She then asks us to sit back and look at her new CD-ROM formatted book, *In Search of Galactic Dinosaurs*.

(Note: an actual school scenario would take much longer, but this abbreviated piece is enough to illustrate the process.)

Figure 3.2. Continued

Once this "visioning" step has been accomplished, the SBM school will have gone a long way toward building support from the community. Unlike a list of education objectives, which often reads to parents like just so much "educationalese," these scenarios make clear the vision sought by the staff. Better yet, they are seldom controversial. Although conservatives and liberals may choose to differ on what is meant by ambiguous phrases such as "critical thinking"

---

1. Ability to make a competent oral presentation
2. Ability to write a complete, original work
3. The development of realistic future goals and aspirations
4. Ability to self-assess and explain strengths and weaknesses
5. Skill in producing quality projects
6. Ability to work cooperatively with others

Figure 3.3. Some Skills and Attributes Demonstrated in the Speakeasy School

or "social skills," almost everyone wants his or her child to look and sound like Ellisa. This is the power of the visioning process. It is getting to a place where all members of a school community—be they patrons, parents, students, or teachers—can close their eyes and see the same picture. Like diverse readers of the same good novel, confusion about purpose, theme, plot, or the major characters never emerges.

Once a collective vision has been authored and shared, the next step faced by the leadership team at an SBM school is consideration of assessment criteria. This is accomplished initially by having the faculty extract "performance outcomes" from their school scenario; this is followed by the construction of rating scales for each outcome (demonstrable skill). For example, the faculty at Speakeasy School could ask themselves the question below in reference to their scenario:

> As we look at our vision for Ellisa, what skills are we seeing her demonstrate for which the school wishes to be held accountable?

In Figure 3.3 is a list of some of the responses of the Speakeasy faculty to that question.

To follow this process to completion, we will examine the way the Speakeasy faculty worked with one of their performance outcomes. Later in the book, we will see how other learning objectives have been attacked by other SBM schools, but for now, we will examine this single faculty's work with just this one objective:

"By the end of the eighth grade, students will be able to confidently deliver a competent oral presentation."

If we are to be credible when assessing our students, we will need to be able to specify our criteria in a more precise way than to merely state, "We know it when we see it." So what is the Speakeasy faculty prepared to accept as evidence of a competent oral presentation? They used a strategy that is becoming accepted in the educational community. It is a method called the rating scale or "performance rubric." Let's stop now and take a look at how and why the rating scale has proved so valuable.

Rating Scales

Perhaps an illustration drawn from outside the field of education will help illuminate the concept of the rating scale. Let's consider the job facing an Olympic judge of diving, figure skating, or gymnastics. Putting aside any political considerations (e.g., Russian judges being prejudiced in favor of their own athletes), one cannot help but be impressed by how closely different judges rate the same performance. It is not surprising to see 10 judges (often speaking different languages, yet using the same 10-point scale) all judging a particular dive within four one-hundredths of a point of each other. Just how are they able to do this?

The way that athletic judges achieve these incredibly high levels of what researchers call interrater reliability is by first becoming extremely clear about which individual traits they will evaluate and the specific criteria they will use in their evaluations. This is done by using what educators have come to call scoring rubrics.

For example, if we were judging platform diving, we might agree that there are four specific traits we want to evaluate: the take-off, the entry, and the mid-air maneuver, as well as the degree of difficulty. We would also have to agree on whether each of these traits are to be given equal weight in our scoring system (let's suppose we agree to that) or to be weighted differently. Because we decided to give each trait equal weight, we agreed that each trait of a dive, if done perfectly, will be awarded a maximum score of 2.5. If the trait is totally absent, then a score of zero would be awarded for that trait.

We could then draw up a developmental continuum for each one of these four "essential" elements. For example, for the trait of entry, we might decide that a perfect score of 2.5 would be granted whenever the diver (a) entered the water at a perfect 90° angle and (b) created no splash.

If these criteria are applied, a belly flop would garner an "entry" score of zero. Judges then define what a mid-level entry would look like (e.g., one that might garner a 1.25 score). When I am creating rubrics for instructional purposes, I look at the mid-level of performance as equaling what we have commonly referred to as "grade level."

Once all the criteria have been delineated, we have our continuum (performance rubric). Still, the clarity of these expectations will need to be tested. This is accomplished by having multiple observers rate the same dive in an effort to create higher consistency (interrater reliability) in scoring.

Applying Rating Scales
to Academic Performance

Most teachers who use the performance assessment process use a 5-point scale for their scoring rating scales (although nothing prevents one from using a 6-, 10-, or even 20-point scale). In our work, we have come to believe that rating scales are instructionally most beneficial for students when they imply a developmental or never-ending continuum of competence. For this reason, when we use 5-point scales, we declare a rating of 1 to mean basic competence (note that a totally incompetent student would be told, "On this trait, you were unscorable") and a score of 5 indicates a fluent performance (thereby allowing for the possibility of further growth). Our rubrics are created by first asking the question, Where would I expect most competent students to be after a successful learning experience? We then specify the observable behaviors or attributes of this student's work and assign this level of performance a score of 3 (as mentioned above, this is what many of us, our students, and their parents know as equivalent to grade level).

Next, we would ask, What would a student's work look like if it was truly exceptional? We then specify what that work would consist of and assign such work a score of 5.

| Basic | | Developing | | Fluent |
1	2	3	4	5
Student has a plan for the presentation	Student adjusts presentation to allotted time	The plan is sequential; it has a clear beginning, middle, and end	The presentation effectively uses media to illustrate major points	The presentation includes appropriate illustrative examples as needed
Student follows the presentation plan	Student appears to be comfortable throughout presentation	The student engages the audience through the use of eye contact and responding to cues	The student elicits and appropriately responds to questions from the audience	The presentation is unified, and the connection between the various components is clear
				The presentation is coherent—it hangs together and tells a complete story

Figure 3.4. Outcome: At the Completion of Eighth Grade, the Student Will Be Able to Conduct a Public Oral Presentation Confidently

Finally, we consider, What would the work be like of a student whose performance was the very minimum one could accept from a beginning student? We assign that performance a rating of 1. The last step is to fill in the scale with the behavior or attributes one would expect to see in a performance rated 2 or 4.

Figure 3.4 is the rubric that Speakeasy created for assessing the skill of "making competent oral presentations."

Once they had created their rubric, the teachers at Speakeasy Middle School had come a long way. They could (using their scenario) communicate their vision of student performance clearly, and

---

Data Collection Plan:

1. Assessment of a videotaped exit exhibition by trained teacher assessors

2. Composite assessments by a lay panel that viewed the presentation

3. The student's self-assessment of his or her exit exhibition

---

Figure 3.5. Outcome: At the Completion of Eighth Grade, Each Student Will Be Able to Conduct a Public Oral Presentation Confidently

they had a rating scale that would help them assess and describe each student's performance across a continuum. But they weren't done.

How could they use their rating scale with reliability? What I mean is, how could they use their scale (Figure 3.4) in a manner that they would be confident was providing them with an accurate picture of each student's true level of performance?

This moved the Speakeasy faculty to Step 2 of the process: planning the collection of triangulated data on outcome attainment. Triangulated data collection means collecting multiple sources of data on whatever phenomenon is to be assessed. Triangulation appears to be difficult because it pushes up against the greatest problem facing all of today's educators: the lack of time! But triangulation need not be overly time consuming. A little bit of group brainstorming often produces an efficient data collection plan with significant validity.

Figure 3.5 is an example of the data collection plan constructed at Speakeasy for assessing students' oral proficiency.

At this point, the teachers at Speakeasy know what they want and also know how to measure it. Are they done? Not quite yet! Remember, the primary purpose of a school is to educate. Speakeasy teachers know they can't expect the kids to arrive at the door competent in oral language. Rather, they see it as their job to use the best strategies to help their students learn or develop these skills. Therefore, one critical question for these educators is, What is the best way for them to teach their students to deliver competent oral presentations? This brings them to Step 3 of the process.

Building Theory

Step 3—articulate the implicit theory (assumptions) about how an outcome is best facilitated (taught)—is a practice that, although valuable, fun, and creative, is often overlooked in school improvement efforts. Theory has been given a bad name in many schools, and what is worse, many scholars have even suggested that theory doesn't exist very prominently in the work lives of many practitioners. To the contrary, I have found schools to be theory-rich environments. However, what is rare in schools is the clear exposition of instructional theory, complete with correlates, antecedents, and understandings related to the theory. Unfortunately, this is precisely the type of analysis that is required, if and when an instructional theory is to be tested through action research.

An approach that many educators have found helpful in making their implicit theories explicit is the technique of "drawing the graphic reconstruction." Teachers often recognize this technique as a close cousin of the prewriting exercise of "semantic webbing" or "mind mapping." It is a process akin to the flow charts used by computer programmers. Figure 3.6 is the graphic reconstruction produced by the teachers at Speakeasy illustrating their theory on teaching the skills of making successful oral presentations. (Note: The specific steps for creating a graphic reconstruction are provided in the next chapter.)

At this point, Speakeasy's teachers can articulate what they want their students to learn, how they are going to assess student performance, and how they plan on building the necessary student skills. They now face one last step: determining if their theory was correct. This calls for conducting action research on the Speakeasy program.

Action Research on Speakeasy's Speech Program

This last step is where the rubber meets the road for a locally controlled (SBM) school. This is because it is here that conflict often emerges. Let me illustrate.

If we examine closely the theory of Speakeasy Middle School (the graphic reconstruction in Figure 3.6), it becomes clear that these educators feel that repeated practice with feedback is essential to com-

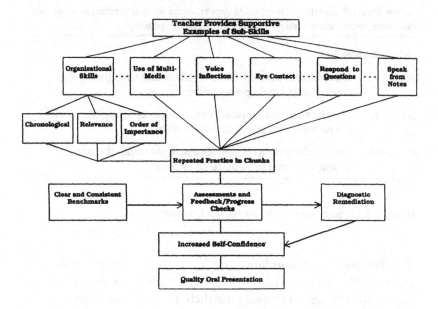

Figure 3.6. Making Successful Oral Presentations

petency development. It is for this reason that the Speakeasy faculty agreed to a most controversial strategy. They agreed that because "practice makes perfect" and oral language proficiency is important, then every teacher should become a speech teacher. Consequently, they decided that students would be given instruction and opportunities to practice oral presentations in every subject: in physical education, art, and science, as well as English and other "academic" subjects. Interestingly, the Speakeasy teachers were willing to do this but only if they had evidence that it was working. For example, physical education teachers were willing to give up valuable class time for oral presentations, but they wanted to see if it really made a difference. And to answer this, they wanted credible data!

This is often the case. People are willing to go along with new programs, but they insist on good data to let them know if the stress of changing was worthwhile.

This, then, brings us to the fourth and final step in the process: the development of an action research protocol for collecting data on the viability of the chosen instructional intervention. As with Step 3,

Action Research Question: Do repeated opportunities for oral presentations in the classroom contribute to student proficiency in public speaking?

Data Collection Plan:

Source #1   Longitudinal data on student self-assessments (using the
             rubric) of oral class presentations

Source #2   Longitudinal data on teacher assessments (using the rubric)
             of students' oral presentations in class

Source #3   Longitudinal data on peer assessments (using the rubric)
             of students' oral presentations in class

Figure 3.7. Sample Action Research Question

this also involves triangulation. Figure 3.7 is an example of a triangulated data collection plan designed to answer Speakeasy's question on the strategy of infusing instruction in oral language.

The End Result

There are many important lessons to be learned from the Speakeasy example. By merging visioning, performance assessment, and action research, an SBM school can take a giant step forward. The faculty become able to articulate clearly what they wish for their students as a consequence of the teaching/learning process, and they have developed the ability to explain and defend the rationale behind their choices of instructional strategies. In addition, teachers in these schools know the educational rationale for their work. Policies backed by data are more readily accepted than those just handed down from on high.

More important, because the data collected by these faculties allow them to act on timely and accurate information on both student performance and the viability of the adopted instructional strategies, continued student success can be ensured. Through the continuous refinement of practice that is grounded in data, teaching in schools like Speakeasy inevitably evolves toward the type of growth-oriented, rewarding, and professional endeavor that hard-working teachers deserve.

4

Reducing the Risk
of School Failure

Few issues command the attention and emotions of today's educators more than the plight of our most at-risk youth. The knowledge that there are certain children who, barring divine intervention, will fail to develop, progress, and meet graduation expectations along with their peers is a source of deep concern for all of us who work with youth. Unfortunately, this is nothing new. Educators, equally as virtuous as all of us, have been troubled by this seemingly intractable phenomenon for years. Despite our collective pain for these kids, we have been largely unsuccessful in designing interventions with much hope of changing what appears to be their predetermined fate. It is that very sorry history that makes the problem of "at-risk students" a perfect vehicle for examining the power of action research and other related accountability mechanisms, as a means to address persistent educational problems.

To see how a site-based management (SBM) school might address the perplexing problem of being at risk, we'll visit the faculty at Totee High School as they "learn" their way through this thorny issue.

Elaboration of a Theory (CBUPO)

One of the organizing principles or beliefs at Totee is that before any issue can be studied adequately by the faculty, the underlying (often hidden) theories that are informing the faculty's perspective need to be fully fleshed out. At Totee, they refer to this as *making our implicit theories explicit*. As mentioned in the previous chapter, one of the often-repeated mantras in education is that a dichotomy exists between theory and practice. Specifically, we often hear experts quoted as saying that universities are places that focus on theory, whereas schools are entities that choose to invest themselves solely in practice.

I find this both a phony and an unwarranted distinction. In all my years in education and throughout my travels, I have never met a teacher whose every action wasn't governed by theory. When I ask a teacher the "why" question, regardless of context, he or she always has an explanation. No matter whether I am asking teachers why they are using the overhead projector, implementing cooperative learning, or using the process of assertive discipline, they always have a justification. They might say, "I am using the overhead to allow transfer from right to left brain," or they might explain a proclivity for cooperative learning because of "a belief that students need to learn to become interdependent," or they might say that assertive discipline "is a means to build personal responsibility." Whatever the explanation, they are reciting for me a coherent theoretical underpinning for each of their professional decisions. In my view, it is slanderous to argue that America's teachers are creatures of habit and not driven by theory!

As said earlier, at Totee High School, they will have none of this slander. At Totee, all discussions of a problem are preceded by a disciplined effort to enunciate all of the implicit theories underlying the faculty's actions or intentions.

At Totee, the faculty achieves this by going through a two-step process. Step 1 is a procedure called creating "priority pies" (Sagor & Barnett, 1994). In the case of their at-risk initiative, the Totee faculty began their work using a process designed to surface their implicit theories. They did this early in October by engaging in an exercise that had become routine at their school—the making, baking, and sharing of priority pies.

Step 1: Making Priority Pies

In early October, all of the stakeholders attended a school community meeting. After some informal chitchat, a cup of coffee, and a donut, each participant was asked to take out a sheet of paper and personally brainstorm a list in response to the following question,

"What are the most significant factors/variables placing Totee students at risk of school disengagement?"

Lori Smith, an English teacher, provided a list containing the following items:

A history of school failure
Lack of parental support
Negative peer pressure
Noninvolvement in activities

Another teacher, Jim Church, a long-time member of the vocational department, saw it differently. His list contained the following:

Low self-esteem
Ignorance of quality
Lack of perseverance
Victimology

After each member of the faculty had compiled a personal list, they all engaged in what had become a favorite part of the process: weighting the items. It is here that they examine their lists and assign percentages that correspond roughly to the perceived power of the factors listed. Once accomplished, the individual lists are then converted (with the help of a box of protractors) into pie charts, hence the name "priority pie."

Jim's pie looked like this:

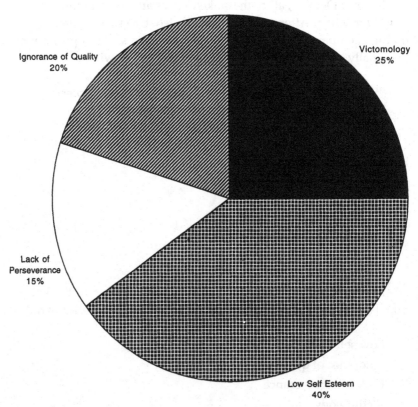

Figure 4.1. Jim Church's Pie Chart

And Lori's looked like this:

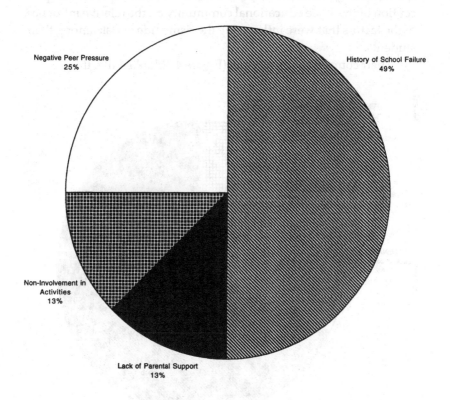

Figure 4.2. Lori Smith's Priority Pie Chart

It is at this point that the process truly becomes exciting for a "learning community" like Totee. Once the pies are constructed, individuals begin sharing them, first in dyads, then triads, and ultimately, with the use of the overhead projector, with the entire group. This is an exciting and enlightening event. Folks notice important issues in each other's pies; they often notice factors that they had failed to consider and thus feel a need to modify their own pies. Others can find themselves in sharp disagreement with their peers regarding the relative importance of certain issues, variables, or phenomena. Although there certainly wasn't quick consensus, the Totee community didn't find themselves too sharply divided on this issue.

As the meeting progressed, several lively discussions ensued, but ultimately, a composite pie emerged, one that captured the perception of the Totee educational community on the relative influence of the factors that were influencing the rising tide of risk among their students.

Their composite priority pie (Figure 4.3) looked like this:

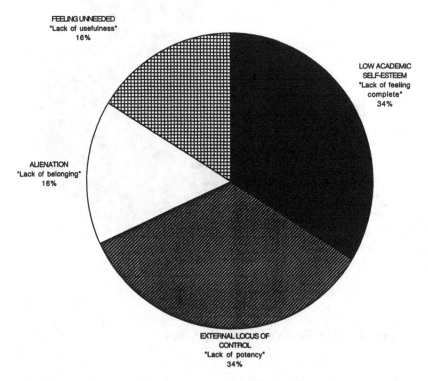

Figure 4.3. Priority Pie Chart: Causes of At-Riskness

With their composite pie finished, they were already feeling a sense of accomplishment. They had not only come to agreement on the factors that they surmised influenced risk among their students, but also reached approximate consensus on the perceived importance of each of these variables. Even the casual observer could see that a "Totee theory on at-riskness" was beginning to emerge. As they ultimately wrote it up, the Totee theory read like this:

We believe that students who fail to receive feelings of competence, belonging, usefulness, potency, and optimism through their school experiences become students likely to disengage from school prior to the graduation of their peers.

They labeled this the CBUPO Theory (Competence, Belonging, Usefulness, Potency, and Optimism).

The satisfaction that came from reaching a shared view of the phenomenon was soon followed by the realization that simply knowing what was causing at-riskness still left them a long way from realizing what they should be doing about it.

Step 2: Drawing the Graphic Reconstruction

Fortunately, the second step in the theory development process was designed to address that precise concern. The reader may recall the graphic reconstruction used at Speakeasy (Chapter 3) to elaborate the faculty's approach to teaching oral proficiency. At Totee, the process of drawing the graphic reconstruction pushed them to dig more deeply into their understanding of the local at-risk phenomena. They carried it out as follows.

The faculty met in teams of five people, and each team was challenged with the same task. They were asked to brainstorm everything they ever knew, considered, implemented, or wished to implement in the name of reducing the tide of at-riskness at Totee. At first, the groups found this task relatively easy. After all, the issue of at-riskness had been troubling these teachers for many years, and their discussions on the topic had consumed hundreds of hours. What turned out to be the challenging part, however, was assembling all of these random thoughts into a meaningful tapestry. The step-by-step procedure that they used is relatively simple, but the cognitive work it called for was quite difficult! This is the procedure they used:

1. *Brainstorming.* Every thought, idea, phenomenon, or issue that comes up during the brainstorming is written on a 2 × 2 Post-it® Note.
2. *Trace relationships.* Once a deck of Post-it® Notes has been created, the team must arrange these diverse items in a way that

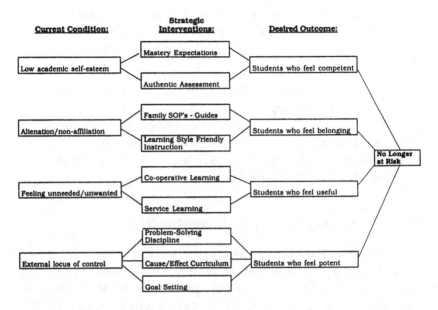

Figure 4.4. Preventing At-Riskness

makes sense. It matters not whether the order is chronological, by degree of importance, or causal—what is important is that the emerging figure expresses reality as these faculty members see it.

Teachers find that drawing a graphic reconstruction is really very similar to the webbing strategies that are commonly used with students as a prewriting exercise.

After several weeks of discussion, negotiation, and reflection, the entire faculty can hope to end up with a picture that expresses their perspective on the problem. Figure 4.4 is an example of the finished graphic reconstruction of the faculty's theory that was adopted by the site council at Totee.

The Totee faculty was pleased with the completion of this part of the project, not only because it made their implicit understandings explicit, but also because their graphic now allowed them to articulate their school policies (aimed at fixing this problem) with clarity to any and all of their constituencies.

For example, they now knew that if and when challenged, a member of the Totee staff could answer a question such as, "Why is the school investing so much energy in pursuit of community service?" They could respond with conviction, saying,

> It is because we at Totee believe that students who feel needed and responsible are more likely to complete their schooling effectively. Because this is a goal of ours, we are using the community service program to enable every Totee student to experience feelings of usefulness.

Likewise, if a faculty member were challenged with the question, "Why are you holding all of the students at Totee to high 'mastery expectations'?" the answer might be

> We at Totee believe that as a consequence of being held to high expectations, children will work hard, meet expectations, and in turn develop high academic self-esteem (feelings of competence).

What becomes most important about completing a graphic reconstruction is not the correctness of the theory but the fact that the faculty understands why they are doing what they are doing.

The reader might be thinking, "All of this sounds great, but what does it have to do with quality control and accountability?" Certainly, it is nice that the faculty have a theory that guides their actions, but what if that theory is flawed, or what if they are seriously overlooking a critical factor or intervening variable? How is a staff like Totee to know? This is why a disciplined process of data collection (action research) is necessary.

The Totee faculty now must review their graphic representation and ask themselves a set of very important questions. The questioning begins with a realization. As nice as their graphic (Figure 4.4) may be, they mustn't forget that it is no more than a set of suppositions. Some of their notions may be correct; however, others are undoubtedly flawed. How will they find out which is which?

Surfacing Questions Worthy of Data Collection

There is only one way to determine what is right and what is wrong about a theory, and that is through the process of inquiry. To begin their inquiry, the faculty at Totee need to look at their graphic as no more than a set of informed hunches. Some assumptions may be correct, and others are probably based on faulty reasoning. How are they to tell the difference? This is done by applying (to the graphic reconstruction) what we call the "two-step test."

The Two-Step Test

The two-step test requires the faculty to ask two questions of each and every assumption on their graphic reconstruction, always keeping in mind that assumptions abound! Every Post-It® Note, every arrow, every single relationship on the graphic reconstruction may be no more than an educated guess. However, because no teacher in America, much less the faculty at Totee, finds the time to investigate every unproved assumption contained in their theories, it becomes incumbent on them to analyze and reduce their graphic reconstruction to isolate those issues/assumptions that are important enough to validate. In short, they need to find the issues that merit the investment of faculty time. The two-step test works this way:

1. Each element of the graphic is subjected to two questions.
2. If the answer to both questions is yes, then the phenomenon merits further study; if not, then it doesn't.
3. The two key questions are
   a. Is this factor/variable/phenomenon significant?
   b. Are we relatively uncertain about this factor's significance?

When the answer is no to either of these queries, then it means either the issue is simply not worth the time required to pursue it further or it is widely accepted as a given. If, on the other hand, a factor receives a yes to both questions, meaning it is a significant factor about which there is relative uncertainty, then it clearly merits spending time in disciplined data collection. At Totee, the two-step test helped to isolate those issues that the faculty "needed or wanted" to know more about.

With the at-risk initiative, the Totee faculty concluded that three specific issues met the two-step test of significance and uncertainty and thereby deserved further investigation.

1. What is the relationship of mastery expectations to the development of feelings of academic competence?
2. What is the relationship of the teacher advisory program to the development of student feelings of belonging?
3. What is the relationship of the service learning program to the development of student feelings of usefulness?

Constructing a Valid and Reliable Data Collection Plan

Now that they had isolated what they needed to know, what remained for the Totee staff was to develop and execute a valid and reliable data collection plan using the action research approach (Sagor, 1992). Although this needn't be an overly time-consuming task, it did require devoting some time to the consideration of sources of data that would confirm or refute the premises upon which their program was developed. At schools like Totee, rather than being concerned with the technical precision of any one of their data collection instruments, the staff invested its confidence in the face validity that would come from the use of multiple sources of data on the same phenomenon (triangulation). Figure 4.5 reflects the triangulated data collection plan that the Totee faculty used to answer their questions about the at-risk prevention program.

A Simulated Report to the School Community

By May, all of the data have been collected and analyzed by the Totee staff. Was this the end of the process? Not at a successful SBM school like Totee! Here the teachers realized that they were in a dynamic relationship with the community they serve. The dialogue on school improvement and educational change for this faculty is ongoing and never-ending. In that context, data collecting and data analysis are only the stimuli for another round of dialogue and communication. As a consequence, members of the Totee educational

Research Questions	Data Source #1	Data Source #2	Data Source #3
1. What Is the Relationship of Mastery Expectations to the Development of Feelings of Academic Competence?	Student Self-Reports (surveys)	Teacher Records (daily work, pop quizzes, homework grades)	Parent Perceptions (phone interviews)
2. What Is the Relationship of the Teacher Advisory Program to the Development of Student Feelings of Belonging?	Student Self-Reports (surveys)	Teacher Perceptions (survey)	Parent Perceptions (phone interviews)
3. What Is the Relationship of the Service Learning Program to the Development of Student Feelings of Usefulness?	School Records (student participation)	Locus of Control Inventory Scores	Perception of Service Recipients

Figure 4.5. Data Collection Plan: At-Risk Prevention Initiative

community (which consists of the faculty, the students, the parents, the board of education, community patrons, and others on the mailing list) were sent the following research briefing:

Good News on the At-Risk Front:
But More Remains to Be Done

In three action research reports recently presented to the site council of Totee High School there was much to be happy about, yet the 3 reports also shed light on some tough issues that lie ahead.

We'll begin with the good news.

Building Feelings of Confidence

As you may be aware, during the past year, Totee students have been held to very high "mastery expectations." All students have been required to complete work at the B level or

---

better or take an incomplete. Meanwhile, extra time and help have been provided for students who needed help to turn their incompletes into A or B grades. This program was begun because the Totee staff felt that all of our students needed to experience the high self-esteem that inevitably comes from doing quality work.

After examining the data of this year-long experience, it was found that:

Eighty percent of the 10th-grade students who had received Ds or Fs when in ninth grade were able to meet the new mastery expectations

Sixty percent of the 10th-grade class reported taking advantage of the scholastic safety net programs designed to help them meet the mastery expectations

Rates of homework completion of eighth graders were perceived as increasing markedly by all of the teachers

Sixty-seven percent of the students identified by the counselors as at-risk showed significant reductions in their at-risk profile

Enhancing Belonging

A second program instituted to improve student attitudes and potential at-riskness was the teacher advisory program. Every school day, our students have been spending between 15 and 30 minutes in mixed-age groups with a teacher who is following them through their Totee career as a special friend, guide, and advisor. This program was instituted to ensure that every Totee student would feel a sense of belonging at school, and we felt that his or her relationship with a caring adult at school would enhance this. Again, first-year results were mostly positive:

Ninety-one percent of Totee students rate their faculty advisor as good or excellent

Every Totee teacher could identify at least one student who benefited from the advisory program

Interviews with parents reflected that 75% felt their children had benefited from the advisory program

Ninety-five percent of returning Totee students elected to stay with the same advisory group

Eighty-five percent of the students identified as at-risk by the counselors reported that the advisory program made Totee feel more like a home to them

Building Feelings of Usefulness

A third program that was instituted this year was the community service program. Each advisory group adopted a service (to the school, other students, or the community) for the 1994-1995 school year. A minimum of 100 hours of out-of-classroom time was expected to be devoted by each student to their advisory group's community service project. Again, most indications were positive:

Seventy-three percent of the students met the 100-hour target

Ninety-five percent of students provided at least 65 hours of service

The school average was 74 hours spent in community service

The cross-age tutoring program (where Totee students tutored remedial elementary students) resulted in the greatest percentile gains ever achieved in our elementary school's Chapter I program

Each one of the 15 nonprofit charities that were served by the service project commended the Totee program and requested our help again next year

Every student who provided 50 hours or more of community service showed an improved locus of control score (indicating an improved sense of personal power)

Eighty-one percent of the students identified as at-risk provided at least 65 hours of community service

One hundred percent of the at-risk students who performed at least 65 hours of service demonstrated improved self-esteem as indicated on the Coopersmith self-esteem inventory

Challenges Ahead

Although all of the above findings were sources of satisfaction for the site council and resulted in our approval for continuation of the mastery expectations, teacher advisory, and community service programs, we have identified some other aspects of our at-risk problem that will require additional attention. Specifically,

Thirty-three percent of the students categorized as at-risk last year are still categorized as at-risk

Thirty-two students let incompletes stand and chose not to take advantage of the services of our scholastic safety net

Twenty percent of the faculty reported feeling inadequately prepared to provide quality advisory services

The faculty and student body are almost evenly split on whether sanctions should be levied against students who fail to live up to community service expectations

Because of these troubling issues the site council has commissioned faculty studies of:

Training needs for the advisory program

Characteristics of students who are avoiding the safety net

How best to manage our community service program

All Totee community members should expect to receive summaries of each of these "action research" reports as soon as they are completed. Any member of the community who would like a full copy of any of the three reports described above (mastery expectations, teacher advisory, community service) should call the school secretary and request a copy.

5

Getting Major
System Changes in Place

Sample Policies, Practices, and
Norms of Behavior

In the previous chapter, we had the chance to meet the Totee High School staff. But in some respects, that was like joining a song in the second verse or entering a party hours after the last guest arrived. It leaves us latecomers with many questions unanswered and issues unexplored.

In this chapter, we will roll the clock back and learn more about schools like Speakeasy and Totee. How did they become data-driven schools? How did they become places where evidence, rather than prejudice, controlled decision making? Was it a result of luck, happenstance, or deliberate planning? Perhaps the biggest question is, "Is it within the power of everyday school leaders to produce schools with the accountability mechanisms that have become standard operating procedure at Speakeasy and Totee?"

Schools like these are not the result of luck or magic, nor are they the creations of people with superhuman talents; rather, they are the living, dynamic result of leadership (often a shared leadership) consciously making efforts to build and strengthen organizational systems that underscore and respect certain basic organizing principles. The belief that underscores all the features of successful site-based management (SBM) schools is that "the staff is made up of professionals."

Professional is a term easily bandied about in discussion, but one that often escapes the deep scrutiny that it deserves. Although it is easy to say that "teachers are professionals," it is also true that the norms and habits of behavior in most schools differ significantly from what one normally associates with professional practice. What, then, are the norms of behavior that constitute professional practice?

There are several essential norms of professionalism that schools like Totee have built into their very infrastructure. Chief among these are the following:

- Professionals don't work in isolation
- Professionals create their own knowledge base
- Professionals take it upon themselves to enforce quality control

It is easy to state such lofty ambitions, but it is something else to create structures in schools that institutionalize and support this type of "professional" behavior. So, what are the systemic changes that need to occur at a school to make it a place where teachers choose to work together rather than in isolation? In many ways, this is the bottom-line question facing folks concerned with site-based school improvement.

In his work with the league of professional schools, Carl Glickman developed a three-part schema that locally controlled (SBM) schools have found particularly helpful when re-culturing their workplaces to better support professional work. I like to think of Glickman's schema as girders holding a strong school together.

A metaphor that I find helpful is the following: Think of a school's culture as its architecture. Consequently, a strong school is built on a strong "cultural" infrastructure that assists the faculty in standing firm against the inevitable pressures and wind gusts (even the occasional hurricane) that often topple many school improvement projects.

We know that the triangle is the strongest of all geometric figures, with each of the three sides providing tremendous support and strength to the other two legs. The same thing holds true for schools that successfully manage themselves. The three legs (according to Glickman, 1993) are the covenant, the charter, and the critical study process. For those of us who wish to create schools like Totee and Speakeasy, each of the three legs of the triangle merits a full examination.

Leg 1: The Covenant (or Sacred Purpose)

It is no accident that Glickman chose religious terminology for this leg. The covenant is an SBM school's raison d'être. It declares the reason for the school's existence and the fundamental purpose behind its work. A covenant goes beyond a mere mission statement, and it encompasses more than a vision. It is a bond and commitment that the entire faculty (and the extended school community) share. Simply put, if a staff member does not subscribe to a school's covenant, then it is inappropriate for him or her to stay at the school. It is not that failing to support the covenant makes a person wrong or less worthy; it's just that being at odds with a covenant puts one at cross-purposes with a community bound by a sacred bond. To understand this, let's consider what a covenant sounds like. Totee's covenant reads as follows:

> Totee High School exists to maximize the affective, intellec-
> tual, and social development of each one of its students.
> While we fully appreciate and recognize their diversity, we
> are constantly striving to have each and every student per-
> form up to or in excess of their highest aspirations.

As stated earlier, if one cannot pledge allegiance to a covenant, he or she is honor bound to seek employment elsewhere. Once a school is satisfied that its faculty is unified behind the same fundamental purpose, the school has one leg of its triangle constructed and in place. But one should keep in mind that a one-legged triangle is very unstable indeed! This brings us to the second leg.

Leg 2: The Charter (School Constitution)

The second leg of the SBM triangle is the charter. The charter is a document and/or set of unwritten understandings that enunciates clearly the system or structure by which decisions are to be made at the school. A charter makes it clear who is responsible for which decisions, how initiatives are proposed and decided upon, and how decisions of the school community will be enforced. In many re-

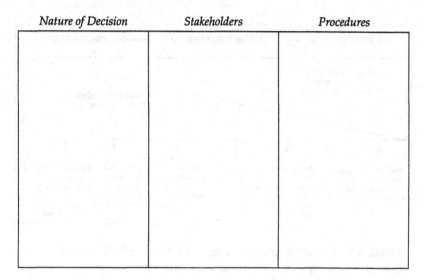

Nature of Decision	Stakeholders	Procedures

Figure 5.1. Site-Based Compact Worksheet

spects, a charter is analogous to a constitution, be it for the American republic or for the student council. In either case, the constitution is an unambiguous statement that helps make carrying out democratic business both organized and efficient. At the same time, a charter must be flexible enough to be amended to accommodate inevitably changing circumstances. I suggest that schools begin the building of their charters by first using the site-based compact worksheet shown in Figure 5.1.

Unfortunately, too many efforts at SBM focus exclusively on the charter, viewing SBM as an end in itself (Odden & Wohlstetter, 1995). These schools fail because they lack purpose. In these schools, it appears that the only reason for reform was to alter the way decisions were made, and the faculty's frustration often runs rampant. Because they are living and working in an unstable "one-legged triangle," teachers in schools with only a charter find themselves forever bogged down in governance but never seem to be quite sure why they are doing what they are doing.

Fortunately, this is not the case at schools like Totee. At Totee, the charter was predated by the covenant. Yes, decisions are made efficiently and effectively, but always with an underlying purpose in mind, such as achieving the school's sacred mission (the covenant).

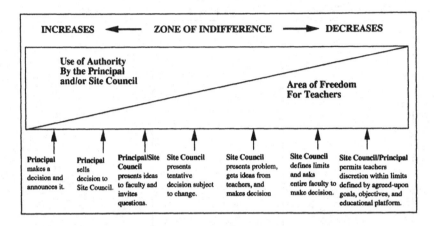

Figure 5.2. Leadership Continuum and Zone of Indifference
SOURCE: Adapted from Tannenbaum and Schmidt (1957).

The key reason for using the site-based compact (Figure 5.1) is to acknowledge and, it is hoped, overcome the most challenging obstacle in all of public education, the ultimate four-letter word: *time*. Experience in SBM schools has shown that many teachers (or parents) are fatigued by their work on a site council, largely because of the ambiguity of expectations. The compact is a way to ensure that everyone who has a stake in a particular decision is involved in the deliberations leading up to its enactment, whereas those who have no significant stake in a decision are free to invest their finite time and energy in pursuits that are more important to their professional lives.

A safeguard that the Totee teachers built into their charter is a simple appeal process that is used whenever there appears to be a misapplication of decision-making authority. At Totee, the principal or site council has the power to assign an issue to any of six decision-making centers based upon their perception of concern versus indifference. Totee's concept of the zone of indifference was adapted from Tannenbaum and Schmidt (1957) and is illustrated in Figure 5.2.

For example, a decision on what color to paint the faculty lounge might be delegated to the facilities committee (based on the assumption that the faculty didn't have sufficient investment in this issue to waste time at a meeting deliberating on this form). However, a decision on changing the format for student progress reports might be delegated to the faculty as a whole. Whenever a member of the Totee community feels that a decision was sent to a less inclusive level than appropriate, he or she can appeal to have the decision referred horizontally to a more inclusive level. This process respects staff time constraints by providing efficiency but also protects the school community from being subjected to overly authoritarian decisions.

Having a covenant (sacred purpose) and a charter (constitution) helps a school to know what it's about and how it will make decisions, but a two-legged triangle is also quite unstable. This brings us to the necessary third leg for successful SBM schools.

Leg 3: The Critical Study Process: Collaborative Action Research

Even with two good legs, a triangle is a geometric figure with no stability. What serves to make a school's infrastructure stable and strong is a third girder—that strategic piece which holds the covenant and charter together. In the case of the locally controlled (SBM) school, this third leg influences the quality of every educational decision made.

The covenant reminds us to focus on issues of central importance, and the charter ensures that decisions are made by the right people in the most efficient and democratically honest manner. Yet we know that even moral people who use fair decision-making strategies sometimes make dumb decisions. The best protection against making bad decisions lies in the extent and quality of the data that inform the decision. It is for this reason that Glickman advised locally controlled schools to have all of their policy decisions informed by valid and reliable data derived from investigations into their own practice. When and where that is not possible, these schools look at research derived from settings where the context is similar enough to justify generalizing and adopting the results as locally appropriate.

An Example

Riverside School has a component in its covenant that states, "We are committed to developing the ability of our students to produce work products which they are proud of and which display an appreciation of quality."

In addition, the charter at Riverside School delegates to the site council primary responsibility for the construction of the annual master schedule and any proposed alterations of the student day.

Consistent with their goal of assisting students to develop the skills and knowledge necessary to produce products of high quality, the site council made sure that action research has been and is being conducted at the school pertaining to the "quality product" issue.

Before the Riverside site council began deliberating on next year's schedule, they reviewed current findings brought forward by their action research cadre. The action research cadre's report illuminated several interesting points:

1. Student interviews and student comments in their portfolios reflected a shared perception that shortcomings in quality were often the result of time constraints.
2. Teachers felt that the majority of student mistakes and oversights on quality issues could or would have been avoided if there had been more active coaching provided by the teachers.
3. Parents reported that their children were producing less than quality work largely because of the school's conflicting demands and the segmentation of the curriculum.

Such information proved extremely helpful to the Riverside staff. They now knew that they were falling short on a critical component of their covenant, and they now had (as a consequence of their action research) the beginnings of an understanding of the cause of the problem. Specifically, they theorized:

Because students were being asked to do too much in constrained periods of time, they were inclined to be rushing to meet deadlines, missing out on appropriate coaching opportunities, and producing numerous low-quality projects, rather than a few significant ones of which they could be proud.

These findings helped to empower Riverside's staff. Their covenant equipped them with clarity about what they were after, and the research let them know how close they were coming to meeting their targets. However, if they stopped at that point, they would stall, stay frustrated, and perhaps even give up. Fortunately, at Riverside, that wasn't the case, because these teachers and this school had, in addition to their covenant and data, an effective charter. They had the means to make good decisions to inform future action. As it turned out, the Riverside site council proposed to the staff that integrated learning experiences be introduced and accompanied by a block schedule, reasoning that if students worked on fewer things while receiving the opportunity to spend more time with their teachers in concentrated efforts on a few multidisciplinary topics, they would be able to use that expanded time to produce products of greater quality.

Armed with these insights, Riverside moved ahead with a new policy and a daily schedule providing blocks of time for thematic instruction. This may not prove to be the "magic bullet" for curing all the ills of low-quality work, but it was an initiative in which the staff could happily invest energy. The decision to change schedules was clearly made to further their mission, it was decided upon democratically, and it wasn't built upon biases; rather, it was the outgrowth of a reasoned and thoughtful review of pertinent local data.

Most important, the parents and students at Riverside had the opportunity to watch the educators "walk their talk." Observing the teachers as learners played a big role in building community confidence in their school. Although the block schedule may not be the ultimate answer to Riverside's problem, it was clearly a smart place to start.

6

Confronting Literacy
Concerns Head On

It is hard to meaningfully pursue a vision until and unless it can be seen and appreciated in its entirety. Looking at the components of a vision is not the same as comprehending it as a whole. When I find myself admiring a beautiful house, I understand that it was constructed of dozens of bricks and boards. However, the picture that I'm looking at is quite different from what I'd be seeing if I drove by a building materials lot and scanned a pile of bricks and stacks of lumber. Managing a school with a vision as opposed to a school without one is the difference between seeing the future or just staring at a pile of raw material.

The value of a shared vision is that it allows us to know what we want our finished products (skilled, successful, and self-actualized students) to look like. The reader will recall the scenario-writing exercise used at Speakeasy Middle School (Chapter 3) to build the faculty's shared vision. But we should also remember that vision setting was only the beginning, because, as we observed at Speakeasy, the really creative work was figuring out ways to arrange limited resources and organize the faculty (the raw material) to transform the vision into a reality.

Although a vision may be shared, clear, and constant, realizing it is a dynamic and interactive process. Students of Deming and TQM

54

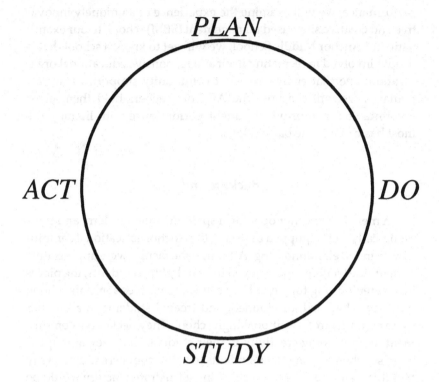

Figure 6.1. PDSA Cycle

may have encountered what is commonly called the PDSA cycle (Figure 6.1).

PDSA is a dynamic process that is used in learning organizations. It assists these organizations in continuously thinking their way through the planning process, undertaking specific actions based upon the planning, and studying the consequences of the actions undertaken so that revised actions can be implemented and studied and improved planning can emerge. Later in this chapter, we will trace the efforts of a middle school as it works its way around and through the PDSA cycle.

There is probably no place in our school curriculum where the need for shared vision is more apparent than in our efforts to develop fully literate students. To illuminate how a school could move from vision to a program that will ultimately result in high levels of student

performance, we will examine the experience of a uniquely innovative and creative site-based management (SBM) school. In our examination of Anchor Middle School, we will get to know a school that is
deeply involved in recreating itself as a responsive educational organization; one that enjoys excellent community support. Most particularly, we will see how the Anchor teachers held themselves
accountable for improving student performance with literacy, the
most basic of all "the basic" skills.

Background

A mere 2 years after opening a spanking new, modern, and tech-
nologically well-equipped building, the Anchor educational community found itself floundering. Although the faculty were appreciative
of their fine facilities and enjoyed their delightful students, the pieces
just weren't fitting together. They called themselves a middle school,
but they scheduled, disciplined, and treated students in a manner
more common to a traditional high school. They declared a commitment to developing creativity in their students, but they attempted
to do so while treating their students to a didactic curriculum. To say
that this state of affairs was producing a frustrated faculty would be
an understatement!

Fortunately, at this point, a new principal entered the scene.
Laura McAllister was known for her success with two other SBM
schools in the Port Columbia School District. Filled with energy (even
if she seemed lacking in common sense), she jumped right in with
both feet and let it be known that her priority was to help facilitate
the school building leadership team (SBLT) in its efforts to actualize
a shared vision that would recreate Anchor as a successful place for
the education of all its students. In a matter of weeks, she assisted this
diverse, 48-member faculty in coalescing around a shared vision (the
strategies she employed were similar to those used at Speakeasy
Middle School). The heart of Anchor's vision dealt with responding
to the developmental needs of each middle-level student.

Figure 6.2 is a graphic that the Anchor faculty produced in the
weeks after Laura arrived that reflected the essential elements of the
structure they had committed themselves to building, the requirements that this structure would place on the teachers, and the consequences that such a program would provide for students.

ESSENTIAL ELEMENTS	TEACHING COMPONENTS	STUDENT COMPONENTS
1. Variety of Organizational Arrangements	*Development of teams/houses to help student achievement *Choices of multi-age/mixed age grouping *Creative scheduling	*Increase sense of belonging *Meet instructional needs *Create a community of learning *Learning process is personalized
2. Cooperative planning/Common planning time	*Integrated/thematic instructions *Use of Gardner's theory for planning and implementing *Team planning for program development and student monitoring	*Connection with real world *Instructional strategies with various learning styles *Core staff for students to identify with
3. Balanced Curriculum based on the needs of young Adolescents	*Focus on the developmental needs of young adolescents-research based *Knowledge about cognition and how students learn, learning styles, multiple intelligences *Learning aligned with core competencies *Balance skill development with content coverage	*Learner centered willingness to gather, organize, and evaluate information *Competency based learning *Project and problem based learning and student needs identified *Success in several areas
4. Exploratory Programs	*Ability to make the complex simple *Provide opportunities for students to experience a variety of learnings	*Learning process is active and experimental *Exploration of several curricular areas
5. Evaluation procedure compatible with the nature of young Adolescents	*Knowledge about assessment to make the transition from just reporting information to using information to provide instruction *Emphasize positive progression *Assessments align with curriculum and instruction *Performance assessment systems and alternate assessments used to improve learning *Standards are well articulated	*Students perform at or above standards *Students learn to use a variety of assessments to evaluate and improve their own work *Students begin to understand strengths and weaknesses

Figure 6.2. Anchor's Essential Elements

Although it is not unusual for a faculty to declare itself in pursuit of a "middle school philosophy," what was remarkable was the distance that the Anchor staff were willing to go in holding themselves accountable for both affective and academic outcomes. Often, when we see a school commit to holistic visions such as "middle level education" or "personalized instruction," we also see a lack of attention to basic academic skills; the trees tend to get lost in the search for the forest. It is for this reason that we will find it instructive to trace Anchor's efforts to create a true middle school while holding itself accountable in the area of written composition. By doing so, we can review a prime example of both innovation and accountability going hand in hand.

ESSENTIAL ELEMENTS	TEACHING COMPONENTS	STUDENT COMPONENTS
6. Continuous progress for students	*Knowledge about cognition and how students learn *Knowledge about specific pedagogy *Knowledge about diagnosis of learning progress *Development of goals in relationship to curriculum instruction, student achieving *Use of building profiles for accountability	*Students become self-directed *Student motivation is increased *Goal oriented, emphasis on essential learning, and academic improvement *Students are able to reflect/self assess *Use of portfolio/profiles
7 Positive School Climate	*Policies, practices and procedures are aligned for the success of all *Develop smaller groups/houses *Develop unity of purpose *Develop communication plan	*Students develop more connectedness in school *Build a sense of community *Increased sense of belonging *Student feel respected
8. Comprehensive Counseling Program	*Proactive practices implemented *Clearly stated expectations *Stress affective Quality School Philosophy *Pursue non-verbal communication skills *Peer Coaching	*Continuous improvement process in place *Quality process developing *Use of conflict resolution skills *Focus on student responsibility and accountability

Figure 6.2. Continued

Anchor's Accountability System

An excellent starting place for any school with decentralized programs that is committed to accountability is employing the procedures commonly called *curriculum mapping* (English, 1978). Basically, the rationale of curriculum mapping lies in the recognition that the only "real curriculum" is the educational experience actually encountered by each and every student, as opposed to the "fictional curriculum," which is the one adopted by the district and/or promoted by the high-profile national commissions. Although these fictional curricula are often quite good, they frequently consist of bold intentions but often are ignored in the crucible of daily instruction. The underlying tenet of curriculum mapping is the belief that the children won't learn material unless and until it is taught to them. In short, mapping is a strategy for "auditing" what the faculty are

ESSENTIAL ELEMENTS	TEACHING COMPONENTS	STUDENT COMPONENTS
9. Varied instructional strategies, student centered practices that are developmentally appropriated	*Instruction is both learner and learning centered *Significant performance and content are identified and in place *Creative Scheduling *Knowledge about how students learn *Integrated, interactive, cooperative research based learning *Research and Technology based learning *Use of divergent teaching strategies *Explore options for special programs *Knowledge of developmentally appropriate practices *Setting of high expectations	*Students achieve core competencies *Students become self-directed, know expectations *Applied technology, use of multi-media *Students take personal responsibility for learning *Actively engage in learning *Project based learning *Ability to work in groups and independently
10. Community connection	*Using community as a learning resource *Continually involve and inform community *Design process to involve parents in educational process	*Students develop a sense of belonging and citizenship *Provide community support/services

Figure 6.2. Continued

actually teaching and then methodically checking to see if anything important has been omitted or overlooked.

Although mapping is always an important strategy, it is absolutely essential when and if a school is implementing a complex, integrated, and decentralized program as were the teachers at Anchor.

Anchor, like many SBM schools, is a place with a bias toward action; here, no one has much patience for long-term, cumbersome processes. Some schools take months to complete a mapping process, but at Anchor, an entire curriculum area could be mapped in a matter of days. For example, when it came to mapping their "real writing" curriculum, they accomplished it this way.

Step 1: Mapping Process

All teachers were asked to write down each of the assignments they were using to teach composition in their classes and at their grade level. This exercise didn't take the teachers very long, and it

E.L. #1 WRITING: Writes effectively, using different forms to suit purpose and audience

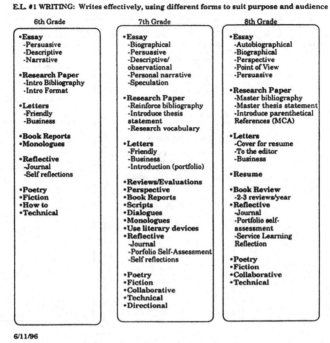

6th Grade	7th Grade	8th Grade
•**Essay** -Persuasive -Descriptive -Narrative •**Research Paper** -Intro Bibliography -Intro Format •**Letters** -Friendly -Business •**Book Reports** •**Monologues** •**Reflective** -Journal -Self reflections •**Poetry** •**Fiction** •**How to** •**Technical**	•**Essay** -Biographical -Persuasive -Descriptive/ observational -Personal narrative -Speculation •**Research Paper** -Reinforce bibliography -Introduce thesis statement -Research vocabulary •**Letters** -Friendly -Business -Introduction (portfolio) •**Reviews/Evaluations** •**Perspective** •**Book Reports** •**Scripts** •**Dialogues** •**Monologues** •**Use literary devices** •**Reflective** -Journal -Porfolio Self-Assessment -Self reflections •**Poetry** •**Fiction** •**Collaborative** •**Technical** •**Directional**	•**Essay** -Autobiographical -Biographical -Perspective -Point of View -Persuasive •**Research Paper** -Master bibliography -Master thesis statement -Introduce parenthetical References (MCA) •**Letters** -Cover for resume -To the editor -Business •**Resume** •**Book Review** -2-3 reviews/year •**Reflective** -Journal -Portfolio self- assessment -Service Learning Reflection •**Poetry** •**Fiction** •**Collaborative** •**Technical**

6/11/96

Figure 6.3. Language Arts Essential Learnings Alignment

took even less time for the school secretary to type up the compiled lists and place them back into the teachers' mailboxes. It then took two short faculty meetings to review the individual lists and to reach agreement on what would be assigned, in which sequence, and at which grade level. These faculty commitments (found in Figure 6.3) were then in a format that could be shared easily with students, parents, district officials, and any other interested parties.

Step 2: Developing an Assessment Plan

When constructing their shared vision, the faculty at Anchor realized that if one of the language arts skills loomed larger than all the others, it was written composition. They believed that it was with writing that students got opportunities to demonstrate their higher order thinking as well as their mastery of numerous mechanical subskills. Ultimately, writing let them demonstrate their ability to communicate complex ideas clearly and concisely. Considering the complexity of assessing such a complex educational task, our look at

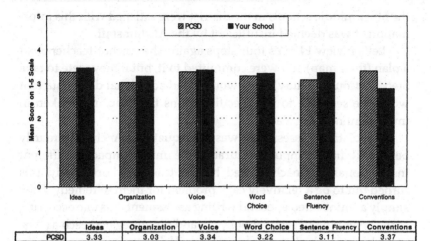

	Ideas	Organization	Voice	Word Choice	Sentence Fluency	Conventions
PCSD	3.33	3.03	3.34	3.22	3.11	3.37
Your School	3.45	3.21	3.39	3.29	3.31	2.85

Means differing by more than 0.3 are considered significant

Figure 6.4. Six-Trait Writing: Anchor Compared to PCSD, Fall 1994-1995

their work on written composition provides an excellent window into Anchor's approach to data-based decision making.

Once completed, the mapping exercise satisfied Anchor's staff that they had at least initially accomplished Step 1 of Deming's PDSA cycle. At this point, they were satisfied that they had a plan (see Figure 6.3).

But how well were the Anchor students actually writing, and in which areas did the language arts program need to be strengthened so that each individual student's writing skills could be enhanced? These teachers had a theory about writing. The Anchor teachers had come to believe that quality writing was built upon the development of six subtraits: ideas, organization, voice, word choice, sentence fluency, and conventions. Equally important, they theorized that these six traits could best be learned and reinforced through the instructional experiences they had outlined on their curriculum maps. The Port Columbia School District (holding a long-term commitment to site-based leadership and accountability) had made available a centralized, well-staffed, and energetic assessment division to assist the local schools. As part of this work, each spring, the assessment division provided each middle school with a profile on every student's and school's performance in the area of written composition. Figure 6.4 is an illustration of one of these district-prepared reports. Whereas the other middle schools in the district were satisfied with this information, it was deemed insufficient by the Anchor staff.

Let's review PDSA's four steps again. The Anchor teachers had a plan (their map) and were committed to it, but if they were to take Step 2 seriously (study), they would need additional data, data that would be sensitive to the specific actions they had undertaken in implementing their plan.

The district's assessment was inadequate for Anchor, primarily because it didn't pinpoint accurately the unique impact of different instructional approaches used by the teachers. Fortunately, this turned out to be a relatively easy problem for them to remedy. They simply administered a second writing assessment, this one occurring at the beginning of each school year, and disaggregated each assessment by individual classroom teacher. Using the two assessments, they could chart the annual growth of individual students (as well as classrooms) and correlate the results with the learning experiences (curriculum) encountered in that classroom by these students. This enabled teams of Anchor teachers to see which of their interventions were giving them "the best bang for their buck." Figure 6.5 is an example of the reports that the site committee had prepared each spring for each Anchor teacher on writing.

Step 3: Building an Action Plan

As the Anchor staff continued to wind themselves around the PDSA cycle, it was soon time to build some action plans from the insights derived from their data. Let's examine how they approached this. In the spring of 1995, it became apparent from their study (the data from their twice-annual assessments) that further emphasis still needed to be placed on the trait of organization.

Three specific planning tools were used by the faculty as they designed program improvements and staff development for the following year. These are generic tools that they use, but we can see here how they helped these teachers strengthen their program in the specific area of organization. Figure 6.6 is a planning tool that provides members of the Anchor staff with significant schoolwide direction. It is a one-page, visual representation of the 3-year language arts scope and sequence (the Anchor faculty created similar pictorials for each of the disciplines they taught).

Figure 6.7 is another valuable tool created by these teachers. It is an example of a "brainstorming graphic" used by one of the eight

Grade	Last Name	First Middle	Student #	Core	Core Teacher	SIX TRAIT WRITING											
						Idea		Organization		Voice		Word Choice		Fluency		Conventions	
						F	S	F	S	F	S	F	S	F	S	F	S
7	Adams	Sam	98003	7n	Jones	5	5	5	5	5	5	5	5	5	5	5	5
7	Bettas	Gail	98134	7n	Jones	4	3	3	4	4	4	3	5	3	4	3	4
7	Church	Marianne	16303	7n	Jones	4	4	3	5	5	4	4	4	4	4	4	4
7	Harder	Cindy	67362	7n	Jones	3	4	3	4	4	4	3	4	3	4	3	3
7	McNeil	Larry	70436	7n	Jones	4	5	5	5	3	5	3	4	3	4	4	3
7	Parkay	Robert	19203	7n	Jones	4	4	4	4	3	4	3	3	3	4	4	3
7	Shoemaker	Jon	70014	7n	Jones	3	3	3	4	3	3	3	3	3	3	3	3
7	Sodorff	Ron	54463	7n	Jones	3	4	2	3	4	4	3	4	3	4	3	4
7	Swoope	Darcy	36303	7n	Jones	3	3	3	3	3	4	3	3	3	3	3	3
7	Young	Michele	43706	7n	Jones	3	4	3	3	3	3	3	3	3	2	3	3

Figure 6.5. Summary of Student Scores for Six-Trait Writing

63

Language Arts Scope and Sequence
Alki Middle School
June 1995

6th grade	7th grade	8th grade
Themes for the 1995-96 school year: •Pride •Honor •Integrity	Themes for the 1995-96 school year: •Pride •Honor •Integrity	Themes for the 1995-96 school year: •Pride •Honor •Integrity

Strands: Environmental Acceptance Social Obligation	Focus: Global Community School Personal

Assessment

•Journal/Daily Oral Language (DOL)
-Done every day
-50% of the time will be spent on DOL, other 50% will be teacher choice (journal, silent reading, etc.) to avoid repetition, stimulate creativity, etc.

•Portfolios
-Process portfolios kept throughout year
-Product portfolio which includes student profile card sent to next level - given to student at the end of grade 8.

Pre/Post Assessment

Daily Oral Language	6 Trait Writing
•every level •September - May •use tests provided •data collection & review for significant educational gains •complete student profile cards for portfolio	•every level •September - May •use tests provided •language arts teachers mix tests, paid afternoon to score •data collection & review for significant educational gains •complete student profile cards for portfolio

Levels Tests	Evaluation Charts
•Reading - Spring - review student gains. Identify areas of concern.	•Use evaluation charts for teachers, students, parents. Include assessment procedures from all three areas

6/11/96

Figure 6.6. Language Arts Scope and Sequence

teams of teachers who collaborate on interdisciplinary units of instruction. This illustration maps a unit built around the theme of "honor" to be taught to eighth graders. Note that this team has committed particular attention to developing student "organizational

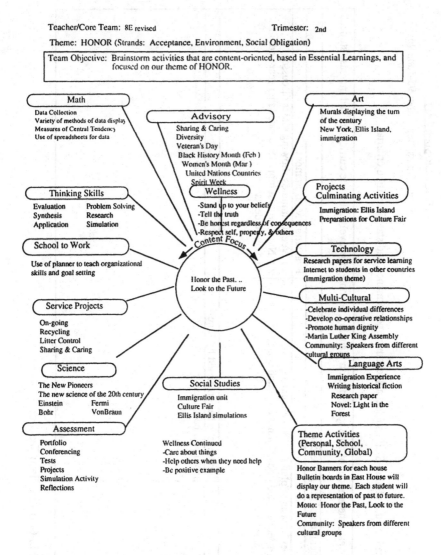

Figure 6.7. Curriculum Integration Brainstorming

skills" by having them write papers involving two fundamentally different genres: historical fiction and a research paper.

The third planning tool is a personal professional growth plan, annually prepared by each Anchor teacher, outlining the areas of pedagogical proficiency they wish to develop. Figures 6.8a and 6.8b are examples of the professional growth plan developed by an eighth-grade teacher for the 1995-1996 school year.

These goals need to be related to our building SLIP, student achievement/performance, and state identified criteria.

TEACHER Sixth Grade
Target Dates, September 95-June 96

INDIVIDUAL GOALS: Increase the amount of time spent in team planning, to more effectively integrate curriculum and increase student proficiency in basic skills.	
OBJECTIVE: Improve integration of 6th grade curriculum	
Tasks/Activities	Evaluation/Measurement
1.)Continue to meet on a weekly basis to plan for common units 2.) Develop a data base of student created book summaries which can be accessed in every 6th grade classroom	1.) Weekly minutes showing topics discussed 2.) Number of summaries created this year and used by students
Data Collected	Findings to be completed by June
1.) Meeting minutes 2.) Summaries on data base	Both will be available

Figure 6.8a. Professional Growth Plan: Teacher

TEACHER Sixth Grade
Target Dates, September 95-June 96

These goals need to be related to our building SLIP, student achievement/performance, and state identified criteria.

TEAM GOAL: To improve reading, writing, and math skills through a program that emphasizes the integration of technology, oral and written communication skills, and critical thinking skills.	
OBJECTIVE: To improve oral and written communication skills, math skills and problem solving skills	
Tasks/Activities	Evaluation/Measurement
1.)Continue to use Daily Oral Language	1.) Improvement of D.O.L Scores
2.) Provide a variety of structured writing opportunities	2.) Number and variety of written projects
3.) Expand the use of technology by the students and teachers	3.) Increased variety of technology used
4.) Provide opportunities for students to orally present material they have prepared	4.) Successful presentation of projects to small and large groups
Data Collected	Findings to be completed by June
•D.O.L. Pre and Post test scores	•D.O.L. Scores
•Lesson plans to indicate use of	•Plan Books
•Technology and variety of written assignments	
•Displays of written projects	
•Showcases where students present material orally	

Figure 6.8b. Professional Growth Plan: Team

67

Assessment and accountability at Anchor is not just an adult pursuit. Each student at Anchor maintains a personal portfolio of his or her work and other school accomplishments. One particular component of the portfolio is the data drawn from the twice-annual writing assessments. The assessment summary sheet that is part of each student's portfolio is displayed in Figure 6.9.

Completing PDSA

The *act* portion of the PDSA cycle at Anchor is illustrated on the team thematic planning charts (see Figure 6.6) and the teacher professional growth plans (see Figure 6.7). The data that are acquired at year's end as a result of the professional growth plans, the student portfolios, and from the writing assessments, give direction to each team and to the faculty as a whole. This cycle is completed each year or whenever a team completes a cycle and begins planning program and thematic units for the next school year. Institutionalizing PDSA at Anchor has made the process of assessing, planning, and doing a seamless pattern of events at a school committed to providing a continuously improving education for its students.

Summary

In the preface to this book, we reviewed findings from Odden and Wohlstetter (1995) regarding three factors that were prerequisites for successful SBM schools:

- Professional development to strengthen teaching, management, and problem-solving skills of teachers and other stakeholders
- Adequate information to make informed decisions about student performance
- A reward system to recognize improved performance

At Anchor, we can see the first two of these features woven into the school's annual cycle. At Anchor, professional development programs grow from valid and reliable data on student performance. Planning routines cause the Anchor faculty to integrate information

STUDENT _____   YEAR _____

SIX TRAIT WRITING ASSESSMENT

	199_		199_		199_	
	Fall	Spring	Fall	Spring	Fall	Spring
Idea						
Organization						
Voice						
Word Choice						
Conventions						

Figure 6.9. Student Portfolio

69

on how well their students are doing and whether or not their programs are producing intended results.

But what is most significant in Anchor's experience, as well as in the other successful locally controlled (SBM) schools, is the functioning of the reward system (the third factor on Wohlstetter's list). We frequently talk about the value of stressing intrinsic reinforcement rather than relying on extrinsic rewards. At Anchor, the intrinsic rewards of teaching are built into the system. The thing that first and foremost bonds the 48 Anchor teachers together is their common commitment to helping their students develop and prosper. That is the reason these teachers went into teaching in the first place, and it is the accomplishment of that goal that has made teaching a fulfilling pursuit for each of them. No honors, trophies, or flags will have much meaning for these teachers if their students are not prospering. Conversely, when these teachers are in possession of valid and reliable data on how well their programs are serving their clients, they find that nothing could bring greater satisfaction.

It is here that we see the magic of the data-based school improvement approach to accountability. Through their accountability system, the faculty at Anchor have put in place a self-renewing reward system, one they apparently never tire of. Their reward is the feedback they continually provide for each other as they collaboratively work through the PDSA cycle.

7

Arbitrating Conflicts
Over Inclusion

A ll too often in education, we tend to assume that we can employ
a "one size fits all" prescription. The reader will recall the discussion of this phenomenon in Chapter 2 when we reflected on some
of the problems inherent in consensus-based decision making.

Consensus-Based Decision Making

Although consensus presents problems for leaders in many ways,
it is particularly vexing for educators for several specific reasons.

First and most important, we know that no two students could
possibly be identical in all their relevant affective and cognitive characteristics; therefore, any effort to fit significantly different individuals with the same cloth will inevitably result in at least one client
whose clothes do not fit. Second, but still a matter of no small concern, is the impact that forced consensus can have on staff morale. In
most other lines of work, when honest professional disagreements
arise over best practice (especially when the data are inconclusive),
alternative explanations and strategies are allowed to coexist. For
example, even in the same cardiac practice, physicians are free to
disagree over the relative merit of regulating diet versus exercise. Yet

teachers are routinely asked to reach agreement on single approaches to many complex instructional issues.

Nowhere do we see the deleterious effect of this trend more profoundly than in the provision of services for our most disabled youth. Few would argue that the treatment of students with disabilities was inadequate prior to 94-142 (the federal law that mandated mainstreaming). However, the argument that any one model of inclusion will work best for all handicapped students is equally unreasonable.

That having been said, throughout North America, we continually witness schools and school systems where a single approach to inclusion is being mandated (not infrequently over the objection of certain parent groups, child advocates, and teachers). Whenever conflict over policy reaches such a fever pitch, the potential consequences can be disastrous, especially for site-based management (SBM) schools.

I believe it is important to note that where controversy over inclusion is occurring, it is usually not the result of evil forces turned loose. In fact, in almost every case where we see inclusion (or for that matter, resource rooms) attacked, we can find good people, equally as virtuous as their opponents, who believe that the other approach is the best practice for students. So, how should a school or district (particularly one that is committed to SBM) resolve such dilemmas? An example drawn from the Hancock Elementary School will provide us with an instructive example.

Hancock Elementary School

Hancock is a good school with a dedicated staff. In fact, it is the very kind of school that most parents would be delighted to have their children attend. All of the Hancock teachers are committed to providing each student with the best possible educational services. Furthermore, at Hancock, there is near unanimity among the staff that disabled children can be best served in the least restricted environment.

For a school that takes pride in being both theory and data driven, it was not surprising that when the Hancock faculty began debating the best way to deliver services to their handicapped students, they decided to start their work with an exercise in the construction of priority pies.

At a school meeting in early November, the following question was posed: "What are the most significant needs of Hancock's IEP

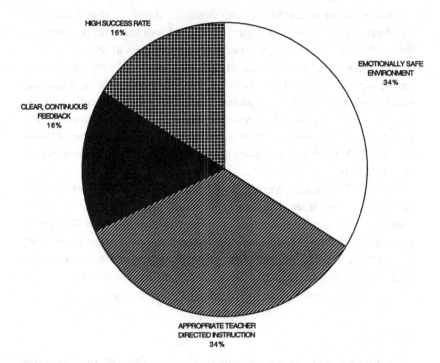

Figure 7.1. Priority Pie Chart: The Needs of Students With Disabilities

[special education] students?" Each participant then personally brainstormed a list of the key factors/variables/issues that he or she theorized were most significant in the educational lives of the handicapped students. Then, the faculty ranked the variables, individually conducting what we call an "intuitive regression analysis." Lo and behold, the Hancock faculty found themselves to be a divided house, coalescing into two groups, with each holding very different yet defensible theories.

Theory 1

One group produced a pie that looked like Figure 7.1. When this group explained its pie, the pie clearly had much face validity going for it. This group of teachers identified two needs as most critical. The first was the need to be educated in an emotionally safe and secure environment. This was deemed so important that they figured it accounted for a full third of the variance. After all, they reasoned, children with a history of failure needed to feel safe and welcome at their school if they were to experience any success at all.

Equally important, they deduced, was the need to receive appropriate teacher-directed instruction. These Hancock teachers figured that because many of the disabled students were profoundly behind their peers, they had a particular need for instruction delivered by a professional who was sensitive to their unique circumstances and who could teach them in classes small enough to provide for individual attention.

Two other factors were of lesser importance (17%), yet seemed far from insignificant. These factors were getting continuous feedback on performance and experiencing a high success rate. The teachers reasoned that if these students were ever to become proficient, they would need to be provided with clear and consistent feedback; and equally important, they would need to experience success repeatedly if they were to believe in their own efficacy.

Theory 2

Although almost everyone saw that Theory 1 (see Figure 7.1) made some sense, there were some teachers who saw matters differently. This becomes clear when we look at the other priority pie (Figure 7.2), which was produced by another contingent of the Hancock faculty.

These teachers saw the needs of the IEP students quite differently. Like their counterparts, this group saw two particular issues looming larger than the others, yet they were different issues from the ones identified by their colleagues. This second group of teachers felt that the greatest needs of the disabled students were the development of an understanding of and respect for individual differences and the development of self-reliance skills.

Their reasoning certainly appeared sound. Because these students were destined to live out their lives in a diverse society—one in which they would regularly encounter people far different from themselves—they definitely needed to understand diversity. It was also clear that they would need social skills and an opportunity to find their unique giftedness if they were ever to become fulfilled when finding their place in the larger society. So, in this second pie, we find another (although quite different) theory on the needs of the disabled student. Interestingly, this one also had a great deal of face

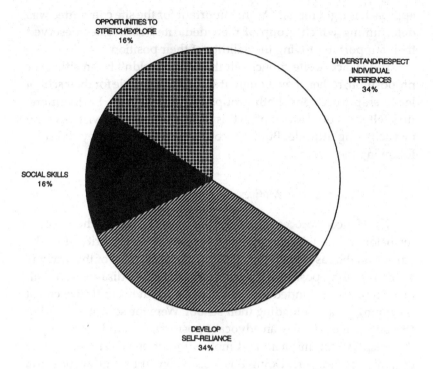

Figure 7.2. Priority Pie Chart: The Needs of Students With Disabilities

validity going for it. If holding multiple theories implies wealth, then the Hancock faculty was rich!

But before the Hancock faculty could rejoice in their professional wisdom they first had to overcome "the one-solution syndrome." This is because a major problem loomed ahead.

Which Program Should They Use?

The first group of teachers, those who believed that the chief needs of these kids were safety and security, could be expected to endorse a strategy aimed at providing "resource rooms" for the handicapped children. On the other hand, those teachers who subscribed to the second theoretical orientation (see Figure 7.2) would be more inclined to endorse a "full inclusion" approach. The question now facing the Hancock community was, "How do/can we determine which

approach is right for us?" More important for the site committee was
determining which group of their dedicated colleagues deserved
their support in proving the validity of their position.

The Hancock site council felt that this shouldn't be an either/or
proposition; rather, they thought it should be possible for their school
leadership to support both groups of professionals. Furthermore,
they felt they could accomplish this without adopting a wishy-washy
or vacillating attitude. But how could they do this? They did it by
following these steps.

Step 1: Establish Trust in Motives

The Hancock process for managing conflicts, such as the one over
inclusion, began with an acknowledgment of the sincerity of all the
parties. In the case of serving disabled students, none of the teachers
was advocating positions for personal gain. Their disagreement, albeit deep, was grounded in sincere beliefs about the critical needs of
the young people attending their school. Were the school leadership
(the site council) to take an advocacy position, it would serve only to
diminish the commitment and motivation of one or another group
of dedicated teachers. Doing this would constitute a grievous error,
for it would squander the most valuable resource available at
schools: the human resource that is the faculty's spirit.

A far better strategy to employ would be the one followed at
Hancock. There, the site committee chair proclaimed:

> We are really pleased to find that two groups of our col-
> leagues have reflected on this critical issue and found
> grounds for honest differences of professional judgment.
> Such an occurrence is clear evidence of the commitment, con-
> cern, and intellectual fortitude of this faculty. The question
> before us is now is, How can we best and amicably manage
> these two conflicting professional viewpoints?

At most schools, the solution to this type of problem is to call for
a vote. Just let majority sentiment determine which is the better strategy for the disabled students. In Chapter 2, we referred to this approach as bias-based decision making and alluded to some of its
negative consequences. At Hancock, they had long ago learned just
how short-sighted such an approach can be. These teachers held to a
basic belief system that contended that the lives of children shouldn't

be held hostage to the biases of the adults who hold power over their future. I think most of us would agree with the Hancock teachers: A child's education is simply too important to be left vulnerable to unconfirmed hunches. The question then becomes, How can leadership proceed in cases such as this one? Having already established trust in everyone's motives, it is time to move to Step 2.

Step 2: Phrase It As an Opportunity

At this point in controversies like this one, the school leadership proceeds with a question. At Hancock, the site council chair said,

> "We cannot professionally make a decision unless and until we have sufficient data to be sure that we are moving in a direction that will satisfactorily meet the needs of our students. So what do the data say?"

In response to that question, it is very possible that one or both groups might offer testimonials in support of their perspective. These shouldn't be discounted. However, it also would be naive to think that testimonials or impassioned endorsements are going to persuade an opposing side to yield its ground. It is far too easy for good debaters to cast reasonable doubt on an opponent's viewpoint. How often have you heard personal testimonials in faculty or school board meetings challenged with statements such as:

> "Their community is different from ours!"
> "Their students aren't as severely impacted as ours!"
> "The values of their teachers are different from ours!"

It matters not what the particulars are of the challenge. Often, it is enough to simply assert that the cases cited do not bear enough of a resemblance to the situation at hand in order to dismiss the argument as irrelevant.

When this happens, leadership has before it three relatively easy choices:

1. Side with one group
2. Side with the other group
3. Say that the issue is so controversial that a logical decision cannot be made and drop the whole issue

Or the leader can take a fourth position (one that is more consistent with Hancock's charter, and having already affirmed the sincerity of both positions). It is to assert that because there is an honest disagreement among professionals, the best approach is to call for a set of comparative field tests to resolve the conflict.

Who could rebut such an offer? If any group (like the two groups of Hancock teachers) truly believed that their approach would help children to prosper, they would certainly be willing to collect evidence to demonstrate that fact. Furthermore, if a group of teachers was concerned that children would suffer if exposed to an alternative approach, the teachers would be more than willing to amass empirical evidence in support of their position.

Such a challenge lays down the gauntlet. It says to the opposing parties, "Can you demonstrate that your position is correct?" If the answer is yes, they will be motivated to try to prove the merit of their position; if the answer is no, they will quickly retreat, and the conflict will cease to exist. If, however, the advocates of competing positions both wish to prove the merits of their theory, then leadership moves on to Steps 2 through 7. This is precisely what happened at Hancock.

Step 3: Commission Pilot Projects

When both groups of teachers elect to continue, those in school leadership positions should take on the role of cheerleader. That is what the Hancock site council did. They continued to express their delight at the commitment of the two groups and backed this up by asking each group if it was willing to test out its theory as a limited pilot project. Again, if one group was unwilling or unable to commit to a pilot project, then the conflict would be postponed, at least temporarily. When both groups wish to engage in field tests of their theories, then the site council should position itself to support both groups. The site council chair at Hancock asked one group:

How can we support you with your implementation of inclusion? Is there some staff development you will need? Are there materials we should acquire for you? We want you to have every chance of success so, while considering that our resources are limited, we want you to know we hope to help you in any way possible.

Later, she told the other group:

> Is there a way we can help you in your effort to give a good
> field test for the resource room strategy? Are there some ma-
> terials that we are missing? Are there scheduling issues we
> could help attend to? Please let us know how we can help
> because if we are to examine this approach fairly, we want to
> give it the very best chance to succeed.

Each year at Hancock, the site council set aside a modest budget that
could be used (at the council's discretion) to support pilot projects.

At this stage, things were proceeding well for both groups. But
before the field tests commenced, there were other things to attend
to. Specifically, how should the field tests be judged? This brought
the Hancock community to Step 4.

Step 4: Establish Performance Criteria

Once both groups had agreed to conduct limited field tests of
their theories, then another task emerged. This was a job for the faculty as a whole: the design of evaluation criteria. Because the entire
faculty has a stake in the success of the school, and because, as a
group, they might possess considerable wisdom on any educational
problem, the task of determining how success will be measured
should be shared as widely as possible.

Following the steps for rating scale (rubric) development described in Chapter 3 (where Speakeasy Middle School designed a
performance rubric to assess its oral language program), the Hancock
faculty went about developing a set of criteria that would be used to
measure the success of the alternative interventions for IEP students.
They decided that the four traits of a good program were:

1. Completion of IEP objectives
2. Improvement in self-esteem
3. Transferability of skills to other domains
4. Parental satisfaction

Agreement was then reached on when and how each of the four traits
would be measured. At this point, the pilot projects were ready to be
launched.

Step 5: Conduct the Assessment

At the end of the pilot project (which at Hancock ran for 18 months), each team conducted a thorough data collection process, assessing student performance on each of the four key traits. This set the stage for completing the last two steps in the process: reporting and action planning.

Step 6: Presentation of Reports

The site council arranged for an appropriate time for both teams to present their action research. At Hancock, this occurred at a well-advertised all-community meeting open to parents and patrons. At the meeting, the reports were presented, and written summaries were distributed to all attendees. By prior arrangement, at least half of the meeting was devoted to questions and discussion among the attendees. At Hancock, reporting meetings are not decision-making meetings; rather, they are seen as "professional seminars." Faculty look forward to these meetings as opportunities to learn about nuances to problems that they may, up until now, never have considered. At Hancock, a month usually goes by between Step 6, the reporting meeting, and Step 7, the action-planning/decision-making process. This provides ample opportunity for folks to consider, discuss, and reflect on the issues and the data.

Step 7: Action Planning/Decision Making

As a consequence of their deliberations on the two action research reports, four possibilities lay before the Hancock faculty. Which alternative would be worth taking would be based upon an analysis of the studies. The alternatives are straightforward and flow directly from the data:

1. *Neither pilot proves successful for these students.* In the unlikely event that this occurs, the faculty goes back to square one: revisiting possible alternative theories on the needs of these youngsters.
2. *One approach (let's say inclusion) proves to be demonstrably superior for all students.* Should this occur, there is no question that while some teachers may be surprised, everyone would be

delighted to endorse this "proven" superior program for full implementation.

3. *The second approach (let's say resource rooms) proves itself better for every category of child.* Again, although we can expect the inclusion supporters to be surprised, being the ethical people that they are, they would support providing this "proven" methodology for all needy kids.

4. *Neither approach shows itself to be good for everyone, but some students benefit from each intervention.* In this case, the faculty realizes that it has grown in its professional development. They have learned more about which types of students benefit most from the two types of treatments. Armed with these data, then, the school would likely agree to continue both approaches, making an effort to consciously program students in the manner that best matches student needs to treatments.

This is precisely what occurred at Hancock. Rather than finding one "magic potion," a single approach that would work for all students under all conditions, this faculty became better at diagnosing and prescribing the right intervention for the individual student.

This end result was fully consistent with Hancock's charter. The Hancock charter contained a guiding policy that pertained to all new program proposals.

Managing Program Conflicts
Through the Charter

To fuel innovation while maintaining accountability, the Hancock community developed a simple yet powerful guiding statement. It reads as follows:

All proposals for new or modified programs will be approved by the site council, providing:

a. There are sufficient funds available, and
b. The proposal is accompanied by data on its effectiveness, or
c. The proposal is accompanied by a defensible theory and a viable plan for data collection based upon adopted criteria.

This policy is prized for several reasons. First, it is positive. In the first sentence, the site council declares itself willing to approve all proposals. Second, it is accountable. Under this policy, no child at Hancock will ever be subjected to an instructional intervention unless the intervention has already proven itself successful or if there is good enough reason to believe it will prove itself successful. Third, it affirms to the faculty that learning is continuous. It is an anthem declaring Hancock's willingness to "learn its way forward."

This policy is one of the reasons that a Hancock teacher was recently heard to say that "Working here is like regularly enrolling in the world's best graduate program."

Gaining Support for
Local Initiatives

Freeing the School From
the Onus of Knowing It All

It is possible that many school administrators will have read this book up to this point with a nagging concern. Passage of levies and bond issues, support of board candidates, and the renewal of the contract of the superintendent are all inextricably tied to the level of confidence that the local community invests in its schools. Although anyone familiar with the workings of our schools may recognize the folly of contending that "we know it all," it is not unreasonable to hold realistic fears about the consequence of publicly admitting our uncertainties.

This is not surprising. We have decades of experience wherein the public has become accustomed to receiving epistles (in the newspaper and district newsletters) on our "adoptions" of the best practices. To worry about the public's reaction if we suddenly declare that on critical matters of pedagogy, we just "aren't sure," will strike true fear in the hearts of many school administrators. But before we accept the wisdom of continuing to model absolute certainty, let's pause to examine the underpinnings of this argument.

A good way to do this is by returning again to our medical analogy. Consider that doctors are professionals with whom we invest considerable respect and confidence. It isn't an exaggeration to say that I bet my life on the prescriptions of my medical doctors. For that reason, it is worth considering how good doctors preface their prescriptions. As I mentioned before, no good doctor has ever declared to me, "Dick, I guarantee that this treatment will work for you!"

Instead, it is far more likely that my doctor suggests a new therapy with this type of statement:

> Hm, Dick, I think I'd like to try this approach. I've had good luck with patients with similar profiles to yours and would like to give it a go. Let's try it for 3 weeks and then why don't you come back for a re-evaluation. If it's working, we'll continue with it; if not, we'll try another approach.

That very comment elicits confidence from me. This is because by taking this stance, my doctor affirms that no two of her patients have identical physiologies. Consequently, she is declaring that what works with one patient will not necessarily work with others. She is telling me that she needs to see how I respond to a particular intervention before she can declare if it is, in fact, a good fit for my needs. Is this the way we approach our students or their parents?

I'm afraid that in too many cases, it is not. Our penchant for adopting the "best" programs has caused us to declare regularly to parents that we have "researched the issue and determined which is the better approach." Be it whole language or phonics, tracking or heterogeneous grouping, assertive discipline or logical consequences, we say we have "reasonably and rationally" checked it out and are now in a position to know what is best for your kid!

One can see why our public has a tendency to be suspicious and distrustful of us. In reality, our physiological selves have far more in common than do the cognitive and affective characteristics of the learners with whom we work in school. Obviously, we already know that students differ. Anyone can tell this just by listening to how often we classify entire groups of children (a whole grade level) as fundamentally different from their peers. Frequently, we can be heard saying things like, "This group of sixth graders is so special, they are such a group of caring and considerate kids." Or, "Wait until you see next year's freshmen . . . they are a group of kids with minds of their own!"

Think about how easy it is for us to classify whole cohorts of students as being qualitatively different from other kids hailing from the same neighborhoods and even from the same families, and differing only by the accident of being 1 or 2 years ahead or behind in school? I think we do this so regularly and confidently because we (like physicians and parents) intuitively recognize that no two children are alike, no two classes are alike, and no two groups of young people can ever have precisely the same needs. Yet knowing this, we still persist in telling parents that we know (with comparative certainty) what is the right answer for their child.

Consider this alternative for a moment. What if, instead of approaching parents with comments like the following,

> Our curriculum committee has reviewed all the available approaches to reading and concluded that whole language is best. That is why we have chosen it for use at Paradise Valley. I'm sure you and your daughter will grow to like it.

we said something like,

> Let's try this approach with Stacey. Now that I know a little bit about how Stacey learns, I think it would be a good idea to place her in Mr. Brown's class. The approach he has been using has been particularly successful with students like Stacey. Let's give it a try for the semester and then see how Stacey is doing. If she isn't progressing by then, perhaps we should consider another approach.

It is a safe bet that Stacey's parents, like me with my doctor, would invest more confidence in those schools that recognize that one size can never fit all than they would with the all-too-typical, assertive, self-assured school that feels it must argue that it alone is in possession of all the answers. I do not wish to overstate a complex issue, but I would suggest that perhaps our insistence on contending that we know, with certainty, the answers to complex questions has been a major factor in undermining the public's confidence in our decision making.

So, the question becomes, How can a locally controlled (SBM) school overcome this?

Inviting Parents to Be Co-Researchers

In the examples offered above, my doctor actually invites and engages me as her co-investigator in her action research on my treatment. She does this by asking me to first approve the intervention. She furthers this process by explaining her hypothesis. Then she asks me to assist her in collecting data, and ultimately, she asks me to help her analyze the data when she asks me if I am satisfied with the progress that I've (we've) made.

Traditionally in schools, we have worked as though there exists a sharp dichotomy. We are the experts on "teaching and learning" and the parents or students are the clients. Is that necessary? The doctor doesn't give up what she has learned through her 4-year medical education and her many years of practice when she invites me (the patient) to be a participant in medical decision making. Rather, she is choosing to add another dimension to the discussion; one that will help to inform our "collaborative" decision making.

A true concept of partnership between school and home changes many things about the client-service provider relationship. In accountable, locally controlled schools, educators take an invitational stance to parent or student participation in educational decision making. By extending choices to students or parents in decision making about all possible interventions, we are seen as interested inquirers into all the areas of relevant data that students or parents possess about the efficacy of potential approaches. Finally, when we solicit their opinions about the ultimate success of the treatment, we are demonstrating caring as well as respect for their role as our partners in the educational process.

One might ask why we have been so reluctant to take this stand. Many will answer that it is because parents value their children too much to allow them to be seen as subjects for someone else's (i.e., the school's) experimentation. It is for this reason that we must take the stigma out of experimentation.

Taking the Stigma out of Experimentation

It is easy to see why parents and other folks have a natural aversion to participating in social experiments. We only go through life once, and allowing our most fragile and vulnerable citizens (our young people) to be the potential victims of scientific inquiry is a moral issue of great weight.

Add to this that when the words "research" or "experimentation" are raised, for most of us, it brings up visions of manipulative experimental paradigms where the subject is either misled about our intentions or kept in the dark about both the purpose of the study and whether he or she has been assigned to the treatment or control group. How many of us would want to be in the group given the placebo in a test of a drug developed to cure a life-threatening condition?

In short, I don't think that this type of research or experimentation has any place in our public schools. It is, in my opinion, patently immoral to withhold an intervention that we, as professionals, think could help a child just because we need to create a balanced control group.

We need to help people to see that research in responsible, locally controlled schools has nothing to do with either manipulation or deceit. It is all about keeping our eyes open and learning as much as possible from what we would be doing anyway were we not choosing to cast ourselves as practitioners or researchers. What we are inviting parents and students to join us in is what has been called *reflective practice*.

Guidelines for Reflective Practice

Confidence

It is inappropriate for us to ask parents or children to participate in a practice that we do not feel in our hearts and minds is in their best interest. Because of this, our inquiries (reflective practice) generally occur in what researchers call "naturalistic settings." This means that what we are actually doing is observing people in their natural environment to better understand what is occurring. The natural environment for schoolchildren is to be in a classroom where the teacher is making use of the best instructional strategies known to him or her. In these cases, the child is not being exposed to anything different from what the teacher would have used with the child had he or she not been a teacher-researcher.

In certain cases, like at Hancock school (Chapter 7), the professional staff at a school is honestly uncertain about which of several interventions is best for the children. If their professional opinion is that an approach is detrimental, it simply shouldn't be used. But if, as at Hancock, two "good" theories seem beneficial for students, and the faculty wish to compare and contrast them, then we are approaching something that is similar to a "controlled experimental study."

Always Get Informed Consent

In controlled experimental studies, scientific researchers try hard to make their control and treatment groups nearly identical. Although that is a nice scientific feature, it should never (for practicing educators) result in our forcing a child to participate in an intervention with which the child or parent is not fully happy. It is for this reason that when examining competing approaches (as at Hancock), parents/students/teachers are given every opportunity to understand and choose which intervention they wish to experience. In scientific research, this is called *informed consent*. Parent conferences, back-to-school nights, and newsletters are just a few of the techniques that can be used to inform parents of all the possible options available to their families. In districts that have embraced SBM, there should already be much experience in how to help parents understand the various options available to them. It is strongly suggested that parents (or the students themselves, if they are more than 18 years old) express their choice of instructional options in writing. This way, there will never be a question about whether they had given informed consent willingly.

As stated throughout this book, offering clients informed choices is a strategy far more likely to build the public's support and confidence in the school than to undermine it. This is because we instinctively trust data gatherers far more than we trust zealots!

Negotiated Trial Length

In the medical examples cited earlier, the doctor always *suggests* a period of time that should be invested in a new treatment before assessing its success. There is a reason I emphasized the word *suggests*: The determination of how long to try something should and must be negotiated. If a parent wants to have his or her child try, say, whole language for only a 10-day trial period and the school believes that 2 weeks is just too short of a period of time to see results, the parent should be so informed. Conversely, if the parent is uncomfortable risking several years on a particular approach, the school needs to open itself up to alternatives. What is, however, essential when making any decision on program placement is the specific criteria by which success ultimately will be judged. This is the essence of accountability.

Negotiated Criteria on Effectiveness

As we saw in the previous chapter, before the Hancock faculty engaged in their comparison of resource room versus inclusion, they needed to agree on the criteria by which they would judge either program to be successful. In our medical analogy, my doctor can tell me clearly and unambiguously what signs we will look for to see if the treatment is working. Similarly, we need to inform all interested parties in our school community about the benchmarks that we will use to determine the effectiveness of competing approaches. At Hancock, they declared that success would be determined by completion of IEP objectives, improvement in self-esteem, transferability of skills to other domains, and parental satisfaction.

Several good examples of negotiated criteria have been presented in the book, such as the criteria on oral presentations used at Speakeasy (Chapter 3) and the criteria used at Anchor Middle School to assess student writing.

Consideration of the factors of (a) informed consent, (b) negotiated trial length, and (c) criteria are important for the decision making of individual parents regarding their child's school program. However, those are not the only research issues faced by an SBM school. The community that a school serves also needs data on how the school is faring as a whole. This brings us to the concept of the school report card.

School Report Cards

Many schools have begun using annual review, school profiles, and school report cards as mechanisms to report to parents and other constituencies about systemwide performance.

One thing that makes "report card" a good name for this type of instrument is that most people already have a good understanding of both the purpose of a report card and what contributes to making a report card helpful.

A good report card tells the student and parent concisely and precisely how well the student is doing; in which areas, if any, the student excels; and in which areas, if any, the student is in need of improvement. Furthermore, most parents/students will tell you that the best report cards are the ones that also provide meaningful narrative comments by the teacher. These comments can be noted in a place where the teacher can discuss his or her perception of which factors may have contributed to the success achieved as well as offer suggestions on how improvements might be accomplished. These same features need to be present in a schoolwide report card.

Items for Inclusion in a School Report Card

When a group of teachers designs a report card to communicate a child's success to parents, they begin by brainstorming the types of data that are important for student and parent decision making. The same process is followed by a school community when designing their school report card. Listed below are the types of items often included in an SBM school's report to patrons:

Norm-referenced test scores
Attendance rates
Grades awarded
Scholarships received
Athletic accomplishments
Activity participation rates
Post-high school matriculation plans
Disciplinary actions
Staff demographics
Budgetary allocations
Achievement of school goals

How to Report on Data

As any parent knows, a report card that consists of no more than a set of letter grades can be very difficult to interpret. What if a television weather reporter gave us his or her forecast using only letter grades? Would we ever know with confidence what to wear? Suppose you heard a reliable report that tomorrow's weather would be a "B." Would you carry an umbrella (for protection against occasional rain showers) or would you wear an overcoat (to protect you from unseasonably chilly weather), or would you simply expect it to be hot and muggy? If we expect our patrons to take intelligent action based upon data, the data need to be more descriptive than could ever be achieved by a mere letter grade.

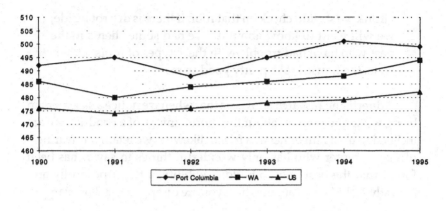

	1990	1991	1992	1993	1994	1995
Port Columbia	492	495	488	495	501	499
WA	486	480	484	486	488	494
US	476	474	476	478	479	482

Figure 8.1. SAT Average Math Scores, State of Washington and National, 1990-1995

One strategy is to report on progress using performance rubrics/ rating scales (see Chapter 3). This way, when a simple numerical score is reported, the reader can simply look at the key (the rubric/ rating scale) and thus be able to tell with precision what the score actually means. Another approach that is frequently used is reporting data over time (so that trends can be observed) and displaying the data relative to a known comparison group (state and national norms). Figure 8.1 is an example of comparative longitudinal data used in a school report card.

Guidelines for a School Report Card

• *Be credible.* Report cards that include only superlatives invite suspicion. In these cases, readers subconsciously dismiss the facts and figures as mere public relations hype. Consider the last time you bought a car. If all the salesman did was extol the virtues of the vehicle—"You will love this car. It is perfect in every way. Everyone I've ever sold one to has loved it."—you probably became instantly suspicious. Contrast this with the experience of seeing a house with a real estate agent who took it upon him- or herself to point out some possible defects.

I think we should check on that roof. If there is dry rot inside, we will want to know about it. I've had some clients in the past who have had trouble with these types of roofs. Otherwise, the house looks pretty good to me.

Advertising research shows us that when we notice a salesperson being willing to own up about the shortcomings of a product, we are inclined to trust him or her as a friend; likewise, we retain our wariness of the promoter who has only wonderful things to say. It has been found that the best way to build credibility is to purposefully and honestly include data about which you are disappointed. For example:

> Unfortunately, 25 senior students did not fulfill the graduation requirements on time.
>
> We were disappointed to find that 12% of the intermediate grade students had three or more disciplinary (office) referrals.
>
> We are very concerned that science achievement scores were unchanged over the past 3 years and still hover below the district average.

• *Be user friendly.* Make an effort to use language that is unambiguous and familiar to your audience. Keep verbiage to a minimum, and keep the document from being too long. One suggestion is consider when and where the report card will likely be read.

• *Remind folks of the school's mission or covenant.* The report card should be designed around the school's sacred purposes (see Chapter 5). This is a not-so-subtle way of reinforcing the fact that the school exists for a particular purpose, and you are "sticking to your knitting." Conversely, if the school contends in their covenant that it has a sacred purpose (e.g., developing the skills of citizenship or promoting lifelong learning), yet fails to report on achievement of or progress toward that goal, then patrons may find a reason to doubt your sincerity regarding the covenant.

• *Reflect your commitment to continuous improvement.* Whereas honestly reporting on your shortcomings builds your credibility, having a viable action plan to remedy shortfalls builds confidence in your leadership. Returning to our example of the real estate agent who expressed concerns regarding the roof line, if he or she had no idea on how to check out his or her suspicion or correct the problem, you would be left wanting another agent. But if your agent said,

"I think we should make our offer contingent on an appraisal from a licensed roofing contractor. I think it will be worth the $100 investment, and I'm sure we can have the appraisal by the first of next week," then your confidence that you were getting good advice would be enhanced. The way to accomplish this with a school report card is to follow your report of each shortcoming with an action plan. For example:

Twenty-five senior students did not fulfill the graduation requirements.

Action Plan: Although we feel that our new, higher graduation standards are appropriate, we are now reviewing our guidance efforts with the juniors and seniors to make sure that all students are receiving adequate help to meet the new requirements. The results of that review will be available in September.

Twelve percent of the intermediate grade students had three or more disciplinary (office) referrals.

Action Plan: We will be instituting a new behavioral management program in Grades 4, 5, and 6 next fall. Whenever a student is referred to the office for misbehavior, the student will be required to negotiate and sign a behavior contract with his or her family as well as with the assistant principal. We will report on the progress of the program in January.

Science achievement scores remained unchanged over the past 3 years and are still below the district average.

Action Plan: There are 10 middle schools in the state reporting consistently high performance in science. We are investigating their science curricula this fall and will be making a recommendation to our curriculum council for revisions in our program for implementation in the following school year.

Recently, the State of Washington, in its effort to encourage SBM, passed a provision in its school reform legislation that requires schools to send all parents an annual report card. Figure 8.2 is an

899 Osceola
Enumclaw, WA 98022
(206) 825-0065
Principal: Robyn Gollatz

SUNRISE ELEMENTARY

ENUMCLAW SCHOOL DISTRICT #216

1994–95 SCHOOL PROFILE

Built 1992
23 Classrooms

Sunrise Elementary was built in 1992. We have 23 classrooms, a large library and a fully equipped music room. The classrooms are built in "pods" to maximize space and allow teachers and students to work together cooperatively. The building is wired for electronic mail to ensure good school-wide communication. Our restructuring focus is on integrating the curriculum. Integrating the curriculum involves making connections between subject areas and the real world to make learning more meaningful for students. To help us do this, our building-wide theme is Discovery, Diversity and Relationships. Units of study have been developed around the topics of "My School, My Class and Me", "The Human Body and Nutrition", "Heroes and Their Cultures", and "Habitats and the Environment." We study these topics by discovering, appreciating diversity, and finding relationships.

	Enrollment			Special Education			Individual Achievement			Chapter/LAP			ESL		
Grade	1992	1993	1994	1992	1993	1994	1992	1993	1994	1992	1993	1994	1992	1993	1994
K	37	35	62	0	1	0		18	12	–	–	–	–	–	–
1st	133	133	128	2	3	6	17	19	22	–	–	–	–	–	–
2nd	136	134	151	7	2	11	13	17	24	–	–	–	–	–	–
3rd	125	141	157	4	8	3	15	5		70	71	74	1	2	4
Total	431	443	498	13	14	20	45	5	58	70	71	74			

Turn-Over Rate	1992	1993
	12%	16%

Free/Reduced Lunch	1992	1993
	21%	20%

Sunrise Elementary Mission Statement

• We believe education is a lifelong process.
• We believe education is discovering and encouraging each individual's potential.
• We believe education is fun, creative, and challenging.
• We believe education helps individuals make positive choices, solve problems, and be responsible, productive citizens.
• We believe education involves students, family, Sunrise staff, and community living and learning cooperatively with mutual respect.

Enumclaw School District:
Working together, committed to quality

• Providing quality educational experiences
• Preparing students for the future
• Involving staff, students, parents, and community
• Responding to changing needs
• Ensuring a safe, caring environment
• Promoting lifelong learning

SOUTHWOOD FOURTH GRADE
COMPREHENSIVE TEST OF BASIC SKILLS SCORER

	Reading	Math	Language	Total Battery	# Tested
1992	57	44	58	53	120
1993	52	47	52	50	134
1994	54	54	55	55	142

FALL, 1994 ENUMCLAW SCHOOL DISTRICT CTBS/4 TEST

Reading	Math	Language	Total Battery
52	49	53	52

FALL, 1994 STATEWIDE CTBS/4 TEST

51	47	50	–

DEMOGRAPHICS

	1992	1994
Read at home regularly	65%	61%
Watch TV 2 hrs or less/day	37%	44%
Computer in the home	37%	55%
Moved into District in last 14 months	13%	17%

Figure 8.2.

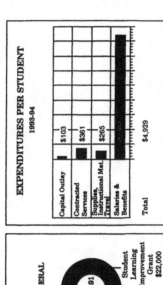

Sunrise Elementary welcomes parental involvement. As stated in our mission statement, "We believe education involves students, family, Sunrise staff, and community...." Working together, we can help our students discover their potential. We have an active joint PTA with Southwood Elementary and we have parent/community representation on our Student Learning Team and other committees. We encourage parents and community members to get involved in their children's learning and volunteer at school as their schedules allow. Volunteers do everything from working with small groups of students to reading stories to helping with parties to field trips to... The list is limitless! The appreciation is bountiful!

Figure 8.2. Continued

95

example of a report card issued by Sunrise Elementary School in the Enumclaw (WA) school district.

Successful schools have learned that community support is contingent on honest, open, frequent, and two-way communication about all of its efforts. In the school communities that have institutionalized these methods of communication, the word *accountability* begins to lose all of its stigma.

9

Bringing Out the Best
in Teachers and Programs

Accountability has had a mixed history in our schools. Perhaps more practitioners see the collection of data, the carrying out of assessments, and the conduct of action research as negative, rather than positive, pursuits. This is not merely a case of mass paranoia. Rather, it can be interpreted fairly as a logical response to a systemic flaw that has plagued our schools: confusion over attribution of responsibility. In education, we have been brought up to believe that personnel are responsible for most everything that happens in schools. We often fail to understand the distinction between personnel and programs and between particular people and the consequences that their strategies have produced.

W. Edwards Deming (1986), the guru of the total quality movement, has argued that 85% of an organization's shortcomings are attributable to institutional practices (the system), with the remaining 15% being the consequence of personnel. Now, let's listen to our own talk. How often have we been heard to say, "It is because of that recalcitrant teacher/employee that the program isn't working," rather than asserting that the data reflect that the program itself or our systems were failing.

For one last time, indulge me in a medical example. If my doctor suggests that I take penicillin to cure an infection, and after a week, the infection has shown no signs of abating, she doesn't feel that she has proved herself incompetent. Rather, she would be inclined to question the efficacy of the intervention she had proposed. I would expect her to say something like, "Apparently, your infection wasn't responding to penicillin. I'd like to try another approach. Let's give Ceclor© a try and see if that works."

If that vignette rings true, you can see that the medical profession has succeeded in separating personnel from practices. This is a lesson we must heed! The consequence of holding on to the perspective that data are a reflection on the quality of the people, rather than the programs or systems, is that it encourages folks to engage in dishonest, or at least less than open, practices with regard to performance data. Much has been written about the negative consequences of high-stakes testing. Basically, if the story found in data will jeopardize people's security or well-being, it is only natural that they might engage in practices to protect their interests, such as by misrepresenting the facts. Here, we can learn something about a systemic attitude from our private sector counterparts.

Let's consider the situation of a profitable and fashionable department store. The bottom line of their profitability will be affected as much by purchasing high-demand items as by continuing to purchase items that aren't moving. With an unhealthy attitude toward data, the store's buyers will attempt to hide any data on overstocks and bring to management's attention only data on the fast-moving items. Such a pattern of deception (if allowed to continue) will almost certainly lead to bankruptcy. Why? Because continuing ineffective patterns of behavior (overstocking unpopular items) is every bit as detrimental to an organization as increasing positive behavior is productive.

Recently, I talked to a teacher who was thinking of conducting research into the efficacy of the particular literacy intervention her district had adopted: reading recovery. I was asked about the "high risk" inherent in her asking whether or not her limited English proficient (LEP) students were prospering in this program. I asked her, "Why do you see this as high risk? Wouldn't you want to know if an approach was ineffective so you could initiate changes?" She readily, but surprisingly, agreed. As a professional, shouldn't she be proud if she succeeds in uncovering data that could ultimately help the children in her school district? I think so. But she was afraid that she might be blamed for bringing to management's attention such a report. This is why it is so important to build an atmosphere of openness and trust.

Driving Fear out of the Organization

Deming mentioned that one key responsibility of leadership was to "drive fear out of their organizations." Nowhere is this more important than in decentralized site-based management (SBM) schools. If staff are afraid that an open attitude toward data will place them in harm's way, then one should expect these people to obscure data and any related facts from their administrators. On the other hand, if personnel feel that data (be it positive or negative) will assist their organization to be more effective, then they will be inclined to become whistle blowers and data collectors.

How do we accomplish this paradigm shift? Experience has shown that attention to certain operational procedures can be helpful in making the change from a person-focused to a system-focused organization.

Operational Procedures

School leaders who want their faculty to assume a healthy attitude about data would be wise to consider a set of procedures to establish this perspective. These might include award or recognition systems for things like:

The insight of the year

The innovation of the year

The uncovered variable of the year

Faculty meetings that feature presentations by teachers on "What I learned while implementing the adopted curriculum"

Newsletters on breakthroughs produced as a result of faculty research and press releases on faculty discoveries

Those who might think that press releases on faculty work are asking the news media to broadcast the mundane, might consider this. Why is it that we regularly read with interest articles in our local newspapers about the latest advance made by medical researchers? For example, it isn't rare to see an article that reads:

A team of scientists at UC San Diego Medical Center recently found that moderate exercise combined with a low cholesterol diet accounted for a 20% decrease in arterial sclerosis in middle aged men.

Yet wouldn't we be equally impressed with the following report?

Teacher researchers at Windermere Elementary School found that when combining a tactile experience such as drama with reading instruction, there was a 30% increase in reading comprehension among students with limited English proficiency.

Local Journals and Conferences

Trade associations and professional organizations regularly sponsor conferences and convocations where state-of-the-art practices are unveiled. The press regularly attends such meetings and reports what is being developed as the next wave of the future. Why not with education? Districts with 500 or more teachers are, in fact, veritable repositories of information on what works and what doesn't. Conferences hosted by local districts could serve as showcases not only of what is new, but also of the capacity of local practitioners to build a knowledge base.

Reconstructing Parent Conferences

In recent years, many schools have seen the wisdom of having their students become full partners in the reporting of student progress. The student-led parent conference is an innovation well worth everyone's consideration. It helps build feelings of efficacy on the part of our students, it gives parents additional insights into the abilities of their children, and it builds metacognitive skills with our students. But this is only one window into a whole world of possibilities.

What if our parent conferences were conceived of as problem-solving sessions—times when student, parents, and teacher could regularly come together to reflect on both what has been accomplished and what challenges lie ahead? Wouldn't parental support be enhanced by a discussion such as this?

Ms. Johnson, I'm truly pleased with Mike's development in the area of creative arts. If you look at the video screenplay he and his partner wrote last November and that his study team produced—My Life as a High School Discus Champ— you will see a very different student from the one with whom we were working last year. His attention to detail, as expressed in his screenplay, specifically the dialogue of the actors, and his ability to tell a story with the use of irony are truly remarkable for an eighth grader.

Likewise, his analytic skills are progressing quite well. For example, the mock "voters pamphlet" exercise he produced showed a real ability to look at a single issue from various perspectives.

As happy as I am about this, I still wish we could find a way to get Mike more motivated to commit to the rigors of memorization. There is a real pattern emerging for him in both math and French. In both of these subjects, Mike isn't doing nearly as well as we'd expect. I believe, and Mike agrees, that this is largely due to his not devoting enough time and diligence to memorization.

Mike, Ms. Johnson, do either of you think we can come up with a plan to address this?

How could we collect data on our plan, and what will be our strategy for reporting and discussing our results?

Such a parent/teacher/student conference follows the same problem-solving steps of fleshing out theory, generating an action hypothesis, collecting data, and reporting results that we've seen faculties using to develop school programs. PDSA works for schoolwide improvement, and it also can work with individual students and their families.

Taking a Systemic Perspective

In the successful SBM school, certain values should already be in place. Specifically, the school community should be of the mind that positive outcomes result from the performance of systems, and likewise, shortfalls also have systemic causes. For this reason, these schools are populated with educators who are inclined to believe that performance can be enhanced by focused efforts to improve system functioning. For schools where those beliefs are in place, the 75% trigger may prove very helpful.

Implementing the 75% Trigger

At accountable SBM schools, it is logical for folks to conclude that if and when the system is working well, at least three fourths (75%) of any targeted group of students (e.g., African American males, language minority females, etc.) should be prospering. This is the heart of the "75% trigger." It is a type of early warning system, not unlike a household smoke detector, whose sole purpose is to alert the school if one of its systems is not functioning adequately. By doing so, the system triggers an inquiry into the proximate cause of the malfunction.

The inquiry process that this early warning system triggers is diagnostic in nature, and the proposed corrections that surface become the school's prescription for repairing the system. When performance falls below the 75% level, it is considered a symptom that a systemic problem must exist. Furthermore, at SBM schools, it is believed that with enough reflection, any systemic problem can be fixed. Examples of findings that might set off the 75% trigger are the following:

Only 60% of sophomores are demonstrating computer proficiency, despite technological literacy being a priority school program.

Thirty-five percent of the sixth-grade girls consistently fail to pass the Presidential Physical Fitness test.

Twenty-nine percent of intermediate grade students received comments on their report card inferring that they weren't working up to capacity.

Although the 75% trigger alerts the faculty to a problem, the ensuing discussion is not focused on who is to blame or on hand wringing about what is the matter with these kids. Rather, it initiates a process of inquiring about what it is in our instructional or management systems that has led to this unacceptably high defect rate. Once a credible answer or answers to that question can be found, then the discussion shifts to what could be done about system change. Invariably, such discussions trigger the commencement of pilot projects, the PDSA cycle, and further data collection on the efficacy of the interventions.

Conduct a Cultural Audit

It should no longer be a mystery that whereas some schools are places where students and educators grow and prosper, others are places where both youth and adults wither. The critical difference between these two types of educational environments is the organizational culture that pervades the school. Jonathan Saphier and Matthew King discussed this phenomenon in a brilliantly titled article, "Good Seeds Grow in Strong Cultures" (Saphier & King, 1985).

Saphier and King use a rich metaphor in asking the reader to look at a school as though it were a garden. We all know that if a garden receives ample sunlight and plenty of moisture, and if it contains soil rich in nutrients, then one would predict that when any reasonable seed is planted, it will grow and prosper. Conversely, if we imagine a garden where the soil was taken from a toxic waste dump, where almost no sun is shed, and where moisture is hard to come by, we would not expect even the best seeds developed by the finest gardeners to sprout, much less turn into beautiful flowers. Saphier and King liken a school's organizational culture to the elements in a good garden. The reason that this metaphor is so rich is because of its inherent truth. It has now been found over and over again that in schools with productive organizational cultures, teachers do their best work and the children are the beneficiaries. Likewise, in schools with negative professional cultures, even the best teachers (those who may have achieved accolades elsewhere) wither or burn out.

Summarizing the lessons from research, Saphier and King identify 12 norms of organizational behavior that characterize schools where students and teachers prosper:

Collegiality
Experimentation
High expectations
Trust and confidence
Tangible support

Reaching out to the knowledge bases

Appreciation and recognition

Caring, celebration, and humor

Involvement in decision making

Protection of what's important

Traditions

Honest, open communications

Through our examination of other research, we have discerned two additional norms that are prevalent in successful schools:

Appreciation of leadership

Clarity of school goals

These 14 norms of organizational culture are the basis of a self-administered survey (Figure 9.1) that SBM schools are encouraged to use.

To conduct the audit, every teacher in the school is asked to rate the school as a work environment to the degree that each norm is a regular part of school life. A 75% criterion is used to determine if a characteristic is truly normative. When at least three out of four members of a faculty see a trait as being characteristic of their school (as shown by a score of 1 or 2 on the survey), then the trait is considered normative. On the contrary, if fewer than 75% of a faculty see this as normal behavior at their school, it is concluded that although this behavior may be something that many people do, it is, nevertheless, not central to the school's culture.

In schools where all 14 norms are in place, we (Sagor & Curley, 1991) have noted that student performance (social, academic, and behavioral) is high and/or improving, and coincidentally, the faculty has experienced success in implementing and sustaining innovative programs. Conversely, in schools where these norms are found to be weak, we found stagnant or falling student performance as well as a poor track record of program implementation.

Figure 9.2 illustrates the profiles of two schools, one that is strong on these norms and one that is weak.

The school culture survey (see Figure 9.1) can be used on a regular basis by any faculty that want to monitor the health of their culture

SCHOOL CULTURE SURVEY

Schools differ in many ways. One difference between schools is the character of their organizational "culture." The culture of an organization can be understood by shared norms, values, and beliefs of members of the community. This survey asks you to think about your school as a workplace and to assess the degree to which each of the following norms or values are consistent features in the worklife of your school.

The norms and values used in this survey were derived from the work of Matthew King and Jonathan Saphier (1985).

Thank you for completing this survey.

Please rate each of these norms or values on the following scale.

1 = Almost always characteristic of our school

2 = Generally characteristic of our school

3 = Seldom characteristic of our school

4 = Not characteristic

Remember! The focus of the survey is your school *as a whole*.

For each norm or value that you score 1 or 2, please provide a recent illustrative example of how that norm is demonstrated through individual or organizational behavior.

Norm or Value	Rating	Recent Illustrative Example(s)
1. **Collegiality** (Professional collaboration on educational issues)		
2. **Experimentation** (Interest in exploring new, not yet proven techniques)		
3. **High Expectations** (A pervasive push for high performance for students and teachers)		

Figure 9.1. School Culture Survey

Norm or Value	Rating	Recent Illustrative Example(s)
4. **Trust and Confidence** (A pervasive feeling that people will do what's right)		
5. **Tangible Support** (Financial and material assistance that supports teaching or learning)		
6. **Reaching Out to the Knowledge Base** (Using research, reading of professional journals, attending workshops, etc.)		
7. **Appreciation and Recognition** (Acknowledgment of quality student or faculty work and effort)		
8. **Caring, Celebration, Humor**		
9. **Appreciation of Leadership** (Specifically leadership provided by teachers, principals, and other staff)		
10. **Clarity of Goals**		

Figure 9.1. Continued

Norm or Value	Rating	Recent Illustrative Example(s)
11. **Protection of What's Important**		
12. **Involvement of Stakeholders in Decision Making** (Those who will be affected by decisions are involved in making them)		
13. **Traditions** (Rituals and events that celebrate and support core school values)		
14. **Honest, Open Communication**		

Figure 9.1. Continued

and to be sure that their school is becoming or staying the kind of place where inquiry, innovation, and accountability will thrive.

Rubric for Program Assessment

In Chapter 3, we introduced the concept of the rubric or rating scale. In the previous chapter, we argued that data on student performance shared with parents in a school report card using the rating scale approach can be a real communication asset.

Up until now, we have been examining strategies and techniques used by schools that have come to see data as their friend—places that have taken to heart Deming's admonishment to credit 85% of shortcomings as evidence of systemic problems, and, most important,

Cultural Norm	Cascade Elementary	Sierra Foothills Elementary
Collegiality	Normative 81%	59%
Experimentation	Normative 86%	63%
High Expectations	Normative 100%	Normative 90%
Trust and Confidence	Normative 90%	45%
Tangible Support	Normative 86%	45%
Reaching Out to the Knowledge Base	Normative 90%	63%
Appreciation and Recognition	Normative 96%	63%
Caring, Celebration, Humor	Normative 90%	Normative 75%
Appreciation of Leadership	Normative 96%	45%
Clarity of Goals	Normative 100%	35%
Protection of What's Important	Normative 90%	35%
Involvement in Decision Making	Normative 81%	45%
Traditions	Normative 86%	Normative 75%
Honest, Open Communication	Normative 86%	45%
	14/14 Normative	3/14 Normative

Figure 9.2. Comparative Cultural Profile

places where there is an ongoing and dynamic discussion with patrons on both progress made and challenges ahead. In schools such as these, there is another use of the rubric that often proves most valuable. It is the use of the rubric for program (as opposed to individual student) assessment. The reader may recall that the six-trait writing rubric used at Anchor (Chapter 6) was based on the view that written composition consists of mastery of the following six traits: ideas, organization, voice, word choice, sentence fluency, and conventions. That rubric was helpful for the faculty in their efforts to monitor the progress of their writing curriculum. In Figure 6.3, you saw how this rubric illustrated Anchor's performance relative to the other schools in the district.

Using Shared Vision in Rubric Development

To get the greatest benefit from rubrics for program assessment, it is important that the school invest both the time and energy necessary to develop a clear, communicable, and shared vision (see Chapter 3). Once a shared vision has been established, the task before the school community is to brainstorm a list of the constituent parts (traits) that constitute the vision. At a school like Speakeasy Middle School (Chapter 3), the school community (parents, teachers, and students) easily could have brainstormed a list of traits that made up their vision. Their list might have looked like this:

Student-focused curriculum
Personalized instruction
Teacher professionalism
School as learning community

Once a set of constituent traits has been agreed to, the task facing the faculty isn't really functionally different from that facing any group designing a rating scale for assessing elements of student performance. The first question to be addressed is, "If we were strong on this trait, how would we know it?"

Let's assume we are at Speakeasy Middle School, and that the trait that we want to assess is personalized instruction. The list of items that might be included as evidence of strength on this trait might read like this:

| Basic | | Developing | | Fluent |
1	2	3	4	5
		Every student has a personalized educational plan.		
		The student and parent participate in the development of the educational plan.		
		The educational plan is built upon an accurate assessment of the student's strengths and weaknesses.		

Figure 9.3. Trait: Personalization

Every student has a personalized educational plan.

The student and parent participate in the development of the personalized educational plan.

The personalized educational plan is built upon an accurate assessment of the student's strengths and weaknesses.

As we see in Figure 9.3, that list of attributes could be classified under the heading "Developing" and written on the rubric as such.

Next, we should pose the question, "If we were a school just beginning to succeed with personalized instruction, what would be the evidence?" In answer to such a question, the following items might surface:

Students' educational programs are developed on the basis of individual guidance.

Student performance is reviewed on an annual basis and reported to parents before scheduling occurs.

Parents have input into their child's program.

Basic		Developing		Fluent
1	2	3	4	5
Students' educational programs are developed on the basis of individual guidance. Student performance is reviewed on an annual basis and reported to parents before scheduling occurs. Parents have input into their child's program.		Every student has a personalized educational plan. The student and parent participate in the development of the educational plan. The educational plan is built upon an accurate assessment of the student's strengths and weaknesses.		

Figure 9.4. Trait: Personalization

These statements then would be added to the rubric under the heading "Basic" (see Figure 9.4).

Next, the faculty should ask themselves, "If we were doing a great job of personalization, what would it look like?"

Each student's program is designed to have a mixture of challenges as well as areas that build on strengths.

Student programs are reviewed on a continuing basis, and revisions are made whenever warranted.

Students would demonstrate pride in and commitment to the work in which they are engaged and in the products produced.

All students would leave school prepared to succeed at their chosen aspirations.

Basic 1	2	Developing 3	4	Fluent 5
Students' educational programs are developed on the basis of individual guidance.

Student performance is reviewed on an annual basis and reported to parents before scheduling occurs.

Parents have input into their child's program. | | Every student has a personalized educational plan.

The student and parent participate in the development of the educational plan.

The educational plan is built upon an accurate assessment of the student's strengths and weaknesses. | | Each student's program is designed to have a mixture of challenges as well as areas that build on strengths.

Student programs are reviewed on a continuing basis, and revisions are made whenever warranted.

Students demonstrate pride and commitment to the products produced.

All students leave school prepared to succeed at their chosen aspirations. |

Figure 9.5. Trait: Personalization

Those factors would be added to the rating scale under the heading "Fluent" (Figure 9.5).

Once this has been accomplished, there is only one step left, which is to determine what discrete examples of this trait could be found and added to the intermediate steps of 2.00 and 4.00.

Prior to being adopted as part of the school's assessment criteria, this rating scale is distributed widely, discussed, and revised on the basis of faculty and parental feedback. Once the site council/leadership is happy with the rubric as a tool, it can become the basis for continuous triangulated data collection and program revision. For example, once each semester, all parents, students, and faculty could be asked to fill out a program assessment using the rubric. Those data then can be shared with the school community (in the school's regular report card). Using this model, all stakeholders would be invited continuously to watch as their school's shared vision moves from "pie in the sky" to reality. This process encourages the entire community to celebrate as accountability and continuous progress become a part of everyday life.

The school that has internalized a devotion to continuous progress truly will have built for itself the essentials of self-renewal; even more important, by making quality control a valued local function, the school will be well on its way toward securing both the trust and support it will need to continue with the all-important mission of preparing youth for an exciting and limitless future.

Epilogue

What About Higher Authorities?

It is certainly possible for the reader of this book to assume that I believe that in a site-based management (SBM) world, we would cease to have a need for state departments of education, district offices, and/or school boards. However, leaving the reader with that impression would serve only to recommend trading the problems of pursuing one extreme with those of another. The more we invest in local control, the more we need to consider and strengthen the critically important roles of policy makers and others who need to exercise responsible regulatory authority. Our nation's democracy was built upon a foundation of checks and balances, and innovative school systems will be well served by following that model.

In Chapter 5, we discussed the building of a school charter (constitution). The technique suggested was to use a worksheet like the site-based compact (see Figure 5.1). The function of the site-based compact was to draw our attention to which people had legitimate interests in which types of decisions and who needed to be involved in which deliberations. When a school system or state system of K-12 education moves into a local control (SBM) model, it is imperative that it goes through a process similar to the site-based compact.

Aristotle, perhaps the first of the great theorists on democracy, suggested that democracy was not the most efficient form of governance and argued that perhaps it was the least efficient. However, the great virtue of democracy that he claimed outweighed its inefficiency was the way it protected the citizenry from abuse. Occasionally, when fatigued by all the pressures we face, we delude ourselves into thinking that in a democracy, what matters are simply the wishes of the majority. But it is always worth remembering that it is the Bill of Rights that first set America apart from other republics. It is in that portion of our nation's constitution that we guarantee the rights and liberties of everyone in our society, whether they are part of a majority or minority, whether they are powerful or weak, whether they have a strong voice or a weak one. Our history is filled with examples where appeals to the central government provided the only avenue open to protect the legitimate rights of minorities. The actions of our courts and central government in these cases did much to advance our society. Desegregation of schools, voting rights, and extensions of the freedom of speech did not always enjoy popular support from the majority of Americans. And without the constitutional authority of central government (often through the courts) to look out for and protect the legitimate needs and rights of the disenfranchised, many critical benefits of citizenship never would have been extended.

The sad truth in America is that all of the schools that our children attend aren't equal. In too many communities, the schools that serve the vocal, advantaged families are clearly superior to the ones serving the poor and disenfranchised. SBM alone can't be expected to cure this. But SBM, along with responsible central administration, can. Let's examine how.

The Right to Local Control Must Be Earned

One cannot overstate the moral responsibility that goes along with local control. Exercising decision-making authority over a child's education can have lifelong effects. Subjecting a particular community (we shouldn't forget that segregated housing patterns continue to proliferate in this country) to substandard education has impacts extending out for generations. Such power should not be exercised frivolously. It is the paramount duty of elected state superintendents, legislatures, and school boards to ensure that every child under their jurisdiction receives the best and most accountable education possible. Simply delegating responsibilities to local authorities won't accomplish this.

For this reason, in the best SBM systems, not all schools are given permission to govern themselves. Local control is something that is granted only to those schools/communities that can demonstrate that they really want it and are capable of pursuing it in an accountable fashion. In this way, every school is given two choices:

1. Develop a covenant, charter, and accountability process that is acceptable to its community (generally this means being acceptable to the site council) and that the governmental authority (the local board of education) is willing to certify is in the best interest of the children.
2. Operate under the control and supervision of the centralized board of education.

For schools that choose Option 2 (centralized control), business simply continues as usual. Curriculum and instruction follows adopted guidelines, and the central office supervises the program to ensure that minimum standards are maintained.

For schools that are operating in the SBM paradigm (Option 1 above), the relationship with the central office becomes radically transformed. Every function that has been provided in the old paradigm—from staff selection to staff development, from curriculum development to textbook adoption, from pupil transportation to student assessment—will still need to occur. What primarily changes is the locus of decision-making authority. At the SBM schools, the power is local, and as a result, the programs that emerge tend to be more idiosyncratic, unique, and contextually sensitive. These unique programs present central administration with the need to engage in a paradigm shift of its own.

The Need to Adopt a Service Orientation

No SBM school will have at its fingertips all of the talents and resources that it needs. Even the best and most accountable of schools will have a regular need for consultants, facilitators, and critical friends. There is no better place for SBM schools to access this type of help than from their central office, county office, or state depart-ment of education. As nonprofit entities, these offices should be able to provide these services in a very cost-effective manner. Because of their experience with a variety of schools, central office personnel should bring broad and enlightened perspectives. However, for this relationship to work, there will need to be a shift in perspective by personnel at the district level. For example, when a service provider answers the phone, he would be expected to say something like, "Hello, this is Dick Sagor. How may I help you?" Contrast this with a regulator, who calls saying, "Hi, this is Dick Sagor. I need to come over to check on your program."

Personnel who have been conditioned to act in the latter fashion will need to learn to adopt the new paradigm, or they will soon find that calls will cease for their services; ultimately, they could even find themselves out of a job.

The best example of this in practice can be found in Edmonton, Alberta. In Edmonton, the size of each central office department is determined by the numbers of calls for service annually received from the locally controlled schools. Therefore, those service centers that are valued by the clients (the SBM schools) thrive, and those that aren't simply wither and die.

There isn't enough space here for a full discussion of all of the issues pertinent to central administration/local school relationships in an SBM context. So, let this one-sentence summary suffice: "It is the job of the central administration to guarantee the conditions for quality, and it is the job of the local school to deliver it." If the local school fails to uphold its part of the equation, then it is incumbent upon central administration to take over.

It is now time for us to seize the wonderful opportunity we have been given. We have the chance to join hands with our colleagues and patrons and begin creating schools and school systems that will not only hold themselves accountable, but will consistently deliver the benefits of a total quality education to all of our children.

References

Calhoun, E. F. (1994). *How to use action research in the self-renewing school*. Alexandria, VA: ACSD.

Darling-Hammond, L. (1988). Policy and professionalism. In A. Lieberman (Ed.), *Building a professional culture in schools* (pp. 55-77). New York: Teachers College Press.

Deming, W. E. (1986). *Out of crisis*. Cambridge: MIT Center for Advanced Engineering Study.

Elliott, J. (1981). *Action research: A framework for self-evaluation in schools*. School Council's TIQL Project Working Paper. Cambridge, UK: Cambridge Institute of Education.

English, F. W. (1978). *Quality control in curriculum development*. Arlington, VA: American Association of School Administrators.

Glickman, C. D. (1988). *Supervision of instruction*. Boston: Allyn & Bacon.

Glickman, C. D. (1993). *Renewing America's schools: A guide for school based action*. San Francisco: Jossey-Bass.

Griffen, G. A., Lieberman, A., & Jacullo-Nopo, J. (1983). *Interactive research and development on schooling*. Austin: University of Texas, Research and Development Center for Teacher Education.

Hargreaves, A., & Fullan, M. G. (1992). *Understanding teacher development*. New York: Teachers College Press.

Holly, P. J., & Southworth, G. W. (1989). *The developing school.* Lewes, UK: Falmer.

Joyce, B., Wolf, J., & Calhoun, E. (1993). *The self-renewing school.* Alexandria, VA: ACSD.

Odden, E. R., & Wohlstetter, P. (1995). Making school based management work. *Educational Leadership, 52(5),* 32-37.

Oja, S. N., & Smulyan, L. (1989). *Collaborative action research: A developmental approach.* London: Falmer.

Sagor, R. D. (1992). *How to conduct collaborative action research.* Alexandria, VA: ASCD.

Sagor, R. D. (1995). Overcoming the one solution syndrome. *Educational Leadership, 52(7),* 24-28.

Sagor, R., & Barnett, B. G. (1994). *The TQE principal: A transformed leader.* Thousand Oaks, CA: Corwin.

Sagor, R. D., & Curley, J. L. (1991, April). *Collaborative action research: Can it improve school effectiveness?* Paper presented at the annual meeting of the American Educational Research Association. (ERIC Document Reproduction Numbers ED 336 864 and EA 023 349)

Saphier, J., & King, M. (1985). Good seeds grow in strong cultures. *Educational Leadership, 42(3),* 67-73.

Schaefer, R. (1967). *The school as the center of inquiry.* New York: Harper & Row.

Senge, P. M. (1990). *The fifth discipline: The art and science of the learning organization.* New York: Doubleday.

Stiggins, R. J. (1994). *Student centered classroom assessment.* New York: Merrill.

Tannenbaum, R., & Schmidt, W. (1957). How to choose a leadership pattern. *Harvard Business Review, 36,* 96.

Tikunoff, W., & Ward, B. (1983). Collaborative research on teaching. *Elementary School Journal, 83,* 453-468.

Wiggins, G. P. (1993). *Assessing student performance: Exploring the purpose and limits of testing.* San Francisco: Jossey-Bass

Index

CORWIN
PRESS

The Corwin Press logo—a raven striding across an open book—represents the happy union of courage and learning. We are a professional-level publisher of books and journals for K–12 educators, and we are committed to creating and providing resources that embody these qualities. Corwin's motto is "Success for All Learners."